A FIELD GUIDE TO
WILDERNESS LIVING

A FIELD GUIDE TO
WILDERNESS LIVING

By
Catherine Gearing, R.N., B.S.

Catherine Gearing

*Cover Painting
and
Illustrations by*
Wayne Barber

Southern Publishing Association, Nashville, Tennessee

This book was
Edited by Richard Coffen
Designed by Dean Tucker
Text set 10/11 Fairfield
Printed on Scott Vellum Offset
Cover stock: Scott Mobile C1S

Printed in U.S.A.

DEDICATION

To my family and many
friends who encouraged
me to write this book,
I dedicate this volume.

CONTENTS

FOREWORD

During 1960, while attending Walla Walla College, I enrolled in the course Campcraft and Wilderness Survival, taught by Dr. Eugene Winters. I found that quarter most interesting and exciting because of this refreshing yet thought-provoking course, and soon I became intensely interested in learning more about edible wild plants.

Since I was a novice, with a degree in nursing education rather than in botany or biology, I hardly knew where to begin my search for more information, but I finally decided to take someone with me who had more knowledge than I to assist me in the identification of plants I did not recognize. Soon my fund of knowledge began to grow, though at first I concentrated upon identification of plants, giving no thought to their preparation as food. Gradually I made the acquaintance of others who had also studied this subject—Pastor Milo Sawvel, then associate youth director of the Northern California Conference of Seventh-day Adventists, and Al Munson, of Pacific Union College, among others.

Hoping to share my newly acquired knowledge with others in at least a small way, I wrote a series of articles on wilderness living for the Feather River Hospital newsletter, "The Feather." Pastor J. H. Harris, then youth director of the Northern California Conference of Seventh-day Adventists, invited me to lecture and display wild plants for a youth leaders' convention in January, 1967. After my presentation, I was invited to give the same lecture and display the following week for another convention of youth leaders. From that point I was booked solid, giving lectures and plant displays in scores of churches all over northern California. Invitations also came in for lectures to garden clubs, to churches of many denominations, and even at Chico State College, where I lectured twice, just a few months apart.

An invitation from Mary Castor Knight, assistant editor of *Life and Health* magazine, to write a series of articles on wilderness survival for that magazine resulted in a series starting April, 1967, and running through March, 1968. From every place I lectured, plus scores of letters from *Life and Health* readers all over the United States, Canada, and foreign countries, came urgent pleas to write a book, compiling in permanent form this valuable information. Many of these letters from ministers, doctors, teachers, and youth leaders inspired me to write. Finally, to my surprise, the book editor of Southern Publishing Association asked me to submit a manuscript on wilderness living for their perusal. Then I knew that I must write the book.

I have given the subject, which started out as merely an interesting hobby, many years of serious study, both in identification of wild edible plants and in their processing and preparation. The research program proved healthful, for I spent many hours out of doors. Every hour I could spare from a busy work program at the hospital I spent in the beauties of nature, endeavoring to identify various wild plants and study their habitats.

In learning how to process acorns and buckeye, milkweed and cattail, and numerous other interesting plants, I used such modern conveniences as the stove, kettles, and food grinder, knowing that learning the principles would enable me to adapt to more primitive wilderness methods when and if the need should arise. I have included recipes using seasonings you will not find in the wilderness just to entice you to get acquainted with these wild plants now, before an emergency does arise.

During the early months of 1969 I became gravely ill—just as I began writing—and at times I felt I would never finish my book. However, my physician encouraged me, ever reminding me of the great need, and urged me to continue writing. In fact, he prescribed that I write at least one hour each day.

My three sisters, brother, and a brother-in-law frequently encouraged me to keep working, and I am sure that without their constant concern and interest I could never have completed *A Field Guide to Wilderness Living*.

I greatly desire that this volume will stimulate the reader to go out into the field and experience, as did I, the thrill of finding new plants, processing acorns so that they become as sweet as walnuts, preparing buckeye as did the Indians many years ago, and learning to subsist off the land should the necessity arise. I feel that this book will be worth all the effort if it will only point the reader to our heavenly Father, the Creator of all that is beautiful and good for us. If it takes the reader into the woods or lovely meadows carpeted with gorgeous wild flowers, if it gives him thrills of discovery which far surpass any TV or other type of armchair entertainment, then I shall be satisfied.

CATHERINE GEARING
Placerville, California

CHAPTER 1

ORIENTATION

LOST!

For various reasons you may find yourself in strange surroundings—you may get separated from your group, or your plane may go down in rugged terrain or in some isolated spot. At any rate, if you do find yourself in strange territory, do not panic and run, for you must conserve your energy. First, sit down and think over the situation. Do not hurriedly decide a course of action. If night approaches, make yourself a temporary shelter and provide yourself with a fire for warmth and to keep away wild animals. Gather enough wood to last the night, and in the morning before you leave, put out your fire completely. It is best not to travel by night, for you can easily lose your way, or put an eye out by running into a limb, or stumble over rocks, or even fall over a bank.

BLAZING A TRAIL

Always blaze a trail when you leave in case you may want to return to your original site. You can use several types of trail blazes.

TREE BLAZE

Chip the bark from the tree until the white wood shows. Two blazes on the side of each tree toward your original site will tell you which way to turn. One blaze on the outgoing sides will do. Blaze the tree at eye level, and each succeeding spot should be clearly visible from the preceding one.

BRUSH BLAZE

Break branches of shrubs about every hundred yards, exposing the lighter underside of the leaves to attract attention. If you make a turn in the trail, break the branch completely off and lay the butt end pointing in the direction of your turn.

GRASS BLAZE

The grass must be tall enough to bind in bunches, using a wisp of grass as a cord. If going straight ahead, leave the heads straight up, or incline them in whatever direction you wish to turn. If the top of the knotted grass points left, the trail goes to the left. If it points right, the turn is to the right.

ROCK BLAZE

Place a small rock on top of a larger one to indicate a trail. Place a small rock at one side of the two rocks to indicate a turn in the trail. A small rock on the right indicates a right turn; on the left side, a left turn.

OVERTURNED LOGS

Use these if none of the above methods are convenient.

FINDING DIRECTIONS

If in a wooded area, climb a tall tree or a high hill and try to recognize some familiar landmark. Look for smoke, for this usually signifies that people are near.

DIRECTION BY SHADOW-TIP METHOD

Find an opening in the trees where the sun shines brightly on some flat, bush-free ground. Drive a stick about four feet long into the earth, keeping it as vertical as possible. Note the tip end of the shadow cast by the stick, and mark it with a peg, a rock, a small stick, or a hole in the ground. On a cloudy day, tap the end of the vertical stick with your finger; the slight movement of the shadow will help you find it. Wait a short time

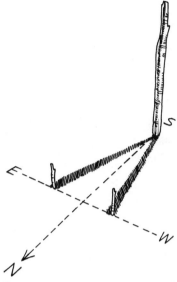

for the shadow to move a few inches. Ten or fifteen minutes will suffice. Then make another mark on the ground at the end of the shadow.

Draw a straight line in the dirt, connecting the two marks, and extend it in both directions. This line runs east and west and the *second mark* is the eastern direction. Next, draw a line from the base of the stick directly to the east-west line to intersect it at *right angles*, extending it to form a large cross on the ground. Mark an arrow point at the end of this line. It points north, and the opposite direction is south, of course.

DIRECTION BY WATCH

If you have no compass but you do have a watch, you can tell directions by standing with your left shoulder toward the sun. Hold your watch flat in your palm. Point the hour hand toward the sun. South is located halfway between the hour hand and twelve o'clock. Use the shortest distance —clockwise in the morning and counterclockwise in the afternoon. On a cloudy day when the sun is not visible, a matchstick or straw held at the edge of the watch will cast a faint shadow. Turn them about until the shadow falls directly along the hour hand. The hour hand will then point directly at the sun. If on Daylight Saving Time, locate south halfway between the hour hand and one o'clock.

DIRECTION BY STARS

Locate the North Star by finding the Big Dipper. The two end stars on the bowl point toward the North Star. (This pertains to the Northern Hemisphere.) Orion consists of seven stars. The star through which a north-south line would pass is the top star in Orion's belt, which sits on the celestial equator. It rises due east and sets due west.

DIRECTION BY NATURE

Moss usually grows on the north side of a tree, although it will grow on all sides of a tree under some conditions. However, do not mistake lichen for moss. Choose trees with fairly smooth bark that grow where the sun reaches them only a short time during the day and that grow in a sparsely wooded area.

Or inspect several trees and take an average. They will have a heavier growth of branches on the south side where the sun reaches them. Tree rings, or annual growth rings, will show a wider growth on the north or northeast side. Take an average of several stumps. Bark is usually thicker on the north and northeast sides.

Some claim that the pileated woodpecker digs his holes in the east side of a tree. Spiders choose the south side to spin their webs because it is dry and warm. Flying squirrels choose east-side hollows for their homes. The tip-top branches of pines, spruces, and hemlocks point southeast. Indians distinguished the north side of a hill because the moist earth made very little noise underfoot while walking, whereas the dry twigs and leaves of the south side crackled underfoot.

SIGNALS

The International Morse Code is universally known. It uses dots and dashes as follows:

A ·—	J ·———	S ···	2 ··———
B —···	K —·—	T —	3 ···——
C —·—·	L ·—··	U ··—	4 ····—
D —··	M ——	V ···—	5 ·····
E ·	N —·	W ·——	6 —····
F ··—·	O ———	X —··—	7 ——···
G ——·	P ·——·	Y —·——	8 ———··
H ····	Q ——·—	Z ——··	9 ————·
I ··	R ·—·	1 ·————	0 —————

You can send messages in Morse Code by lantern, flashlight, torch, whistle, or a mirror using the sun's reflection. Always pause and count three when you end each letter, and count five at the end of each sentence.

SMUDGE FIRE SIGNAL

A smudge fire can serve as a smoke signal. Three of anything—three rocks, three clumps of grass, three smudge fires, three blazes on a tree, or three gunshots—have always designated distress or danger. In using the smudge fire, build three fires far enough apart to be distinguished at a distance. Pile on wet leaves, green branches, or anything that will make the fire smoke. If you are in snow country, a message of distress—S O S— can be formed on the snow with evergreen boughs. Make the letters large. If no boughs are available, tramp the snow, making large letters.

FOLLOWING STREAMS

Following streams can prove a mixed blessing. Usually following a stream downhill will eventually lead back to civilization if it is in well-settled country. However, you must realize that the stream might end in an isolated pond or take you even farther away from where you would like to go. Sometimes a stream is hard to follow because of thick vegetation, waterfalls, cliffs, or side canyons, and detours could cost you many weary hours plus physical exhaustion. In flat country the stream may meander or drain into swamps or thick vegetation. On the other hand, a stream *may* lead to inhabited areas and will give you a good source of food and water.

CHAPTER 2

WATER

GENERAL INFORMATION

You can live for weeks without food, but you can survive only about a week without water. The body needs two quarts of water a day, but you can get along temporarily with as little as a quart a day. If your water supply is limited, sip small amounts frequently. If you are thirsty and suddenly come upon a water supply, do not drink a large amount of water at once, but sip slowly. Avoid drinking very cold water. Warm it in your mouth before swallowing it. If you have an ample supply of water and plan on going into arid country, drink all you can hold before leaving, using your body as a reservoir.

CONSERVING BODY FLUIDS

If you take less than a quart of water with you, avoid starchy or highly seasoned foods. Eating increases thirst. The less activity you engage in, the less water you will need. The more you perspire, either due to heat or hard work, the more water you will lose and the more you will need to drink.

PURIFYING WATER

All water should come from a pure source, and you cannot judge the purity of the water by its looks. The decaying body of an animal upstream can make beautifully clear, sparkling water impure. On the other hand, muddy water may be absolutely free from bacteria. Some of the dangers lurking in impure water are dysentery, cholera, typhoid, flukes, worms, and leeches. If in doubt as to the purity of the water, boil it, for boiling destroys most bacteria. At sea level, boil the water for five minutes. For every additional thousand feet of altitude, increase the boiling time by one minute. For example, at four thousand feet elevation, boil the water for nine minutes. At six thousand feet, boil it for eleven minutes. To make the water taste better after boiling it, aerate it by pouring it back and forth from one vessel to another.

Halizone water-purifying tablets depend on the release of chlorine gas. Therefore, if used, these tablets should be fresh. Keep the bottle tightly closed, with some cotton in it to absorb the moisture. Use two Halizone tablets to a quart of water. Let it stand for thirty minutes. If the water is muddy or if you have reason to believe the water is highly contaminated, double the amount of Halizone and let it stand for one hour.

You can use iodine as a water purifier by dropping three or four drops into a quart of water and letting it stand for thirty minutes. Iodine Purification Tablets are also available. Use one tablet to a quart of water, and let it stand for thirty minutes. Laundry bleach, two drops to a quart of water, is commonly used. Let it stand for thirty minutes before using.

FILTERING AND DEODORIZING WATER

Filter muddy or stagnant water. You can make a wilderness filter by scooping out a hole a few feet from the main water supply and using the water that seeps into it. Of course, you may filter the water through a clean cloth. Water can be deodorized by dropping small amounts of charcoal into boiling water. If you do not have any charcoal with you, drop several small chunks of charred hardwood from your campfire into the boiling water. Let it simmer fifteen to twenty minutes, and strain the water. If you have plenty of time, let it settle to the bottom of the vessel, then carefully pour the water off.

INDICATIONS OF WATER

When trying to find water, watch the activity of birds and animals, because they must have water, too. The chirping of birds in semiarid brush country usually means that water is near. Birds will circle over a water hole in desert areas. Runways and trails of animals may lead to water. A reliable indication is a progressive deepening and widening of game trails. This welcome sign usually indicates that water is near. Salt grass, rushes, cattails, willows, greasewood, sedges, and elderberries grow where water lies close to the surface.

GROUND WATER

In rocky ground look for springs and seepages. The best springs are usually found in lava rock or limestone, although springs and seepages may also be found in clay, gravel, and sand. Dig in dry stream beds. Look for a wet place on the surface of a clay bluff or a wet spot at its base, and dig for water. Let it seep in. Lush, green grassy areas along hillsides indicate that water lies near the surface. Dig a ditch at the base of the patch of green. Be sure to wait for the water to seep in. If spring water is cold, it is usually safe. Beware of warm water, as it is likely polluted. If you have to dig for water, remember that the water table is usually close to the surface in low forested areas, along the seashore, and along dry riverbeds.

WATER ALONG THE SEASHORE

If stranded by the seashore, do not drink sea water. It has a high concentration of sodium and magnesium salts. The body's attempt to eliminate these salts will draw fluid from the tissues, and the kidneys will eventually fail. Never drink urine. The salt content is too high. Scoop out holes in the sand at low tide. The farther away from the ocean, the fresher the water will be, but you will have to work harder to get it. Do not dig too deeply close to the sea. The first water to seep in will be fresh, since it is lighter than salt water. The deeper you dig, the saltier it will get.

WATER IN THE DESERT

If you should come across a desert lake which has a high concentration of salt, dig a hole in the first depression behind the first sand dune. The minute you strike wet sand, stop. Wait for the water to seep in. It will be fresh enough to be drinkable. If you find no desert lakes where you are, pick the lowest point between sand dunes, and dig down about five or six feet. If you come to damp sand, keep digging until you find water. Remember to wait for the water to seep in.

Watch the flight of pigeons or parrots in early morning and late evening. They will be seeking water.

The barrel cactus is a good source of water in the desert. To get water from this plant, cut off the top and mash or pulverize the pulp inside. Water will ooze out and collect in the bowl of the plant. Dip it out, or cut a hole in the side toward the bottom and let it drip into a vessel. You may quench your thirst by eating cactus apples or prickly pears. Cactus pads are edible and juicy. You can also roast them and eat them to help quench your thirst.

In the desert you will need a minimum of four quarts of water a day. Remember that heat and activity increase your need for water. Travel in the cool of the night, and keep in the shade as much as possible in the daytime. Keep your clothes on. Without clothing, sweat evaporates fast, and you will also get severely sunburned.

When you sit down in the desert, squat a few inches above the ground, for it may be as much as thirty degrees cooler one foot above the ground. This will save a lot of perspiration loss, and you will feel more comfortable. Slow motion is the rule in the hot desert, for it requires much less water intake.

You can collect dew in the desert by digging a hole, lining it with canvas, an animal skin, or whatever you may have that will hold water. Line the canvas with pebbles which have been dug at least a foot or more underground. Dew will collect on the pebbles and trickle down onto the canvas. Do this early in the morning. You can also take a piece of clean cloth and mop up dew from stones, covers of tin, or from small desert plants. Some have mopped up as much as a quart of dew in an hour.

WATER HOLES

It is important to know how to recognize poisonous water holes. In desert areas, some water holes contain such poisons as arsenic. Look around for bones of luckless animals nearby. An almost sure way to tell a poisonous water hole is the conspicuous absence of green vegetation. Avoid all water holes, therefore, which do not have green plants growing around them.

SNOW AND ICE WATER

Snow can be melted for water, but remember that ice will yield more water than snow. If stranded on the ocean where ice is present, you should know that ice becomes fresh during the period between its formation and the end of the first summer thereafter. Ice from ocean salt water will be almost perfectly fresh in one year, and in two years will be as fresh as river ice. One way to distinguish between old ice and new is by color. Old ice has a bluish cast to it and rounded corners. New sea ice is gray, milky, and hard.

WATER BY CONDENSATION

While stranded on the ocean, if you happen to have a large covered metal container and a lantern, you may get water by condensation. Remove the lid of your metal container and submerge the closed end in a foot or more of salt water. Place the lighted lantern inside the container, on the bottom. Cover the open top of the container, allowing only enough air to enter to keep the lantern burning. Heat from the lantern will cause moisture to form on the inside of the container. You can soak this up with a clean cloth and squeeze it into a cup or whatever container you may have available. The Air Force suggests this method.

WATER FROM PLANTS

Succulent plant tissues provide a source of water when eaten. Vines, stems, and fruits are valuable sources of water. Large grapevines will yield water in the summer and fall. To tap a grapevine, reach as high as you can and cut off the vine. Then cut the vine off close to the ground. Let the water drip from the lower end, and catch it in a container. When it stops dripping, cut another section off the top of the vine, and more water will drain out. Do NOT cut the bottom of the vine first, for you will lose all the water from the vine as it ascends the vine and spills out over the top.

Bamboo is another fairly good source of water. Shake a stem of old, yellowish bamboo. If it gurgles, cut a notch at the base of each joint and catch the water. Some palm trees have a drinkable, sugary sap. This is true of the coconut, sugar, and other palms. Coconuts have liquid in them that is best when the nuts are green. The green nut has more fluid and will not harm you. If you drink more than four cups of *ripe* coconut juice in one day, it will act as a violent physic. The astringent water from the trunk of young banana trees is drinkable. Beware of cactuslike plants with milky sap.

CHAPTER 3

FOOD

Water is probably more important than food, yet one must be able to identify wild edible plants when stranded in the wilderness if he is to survive over a long period of time. With a little study, many of these valuable plants can be recognized and gathered almost anywhere you may go. Nature provides an abundance of wild fruits, nuts, buds, blossoms, leaves, stems, sprouts, tubers, bulbs, and seeds. You will not find all of these, however, in one place or in any one season of the year.

Do not panic if you find yourself without a food supply. Remember that if you have water, you may live for many days without food. Always watch for wild foods even if you have a small supply of food on hand. If your water supply is low, avoid dry, starchy, highly flavored foods, or meat. If you have plenty of water, eat foods high in carbohydrates. Do not overexert yourself. The less you work or expend your energy, the less food and water you will require. Aim for two meals a day, one of which is hot. Remember that cooking makes food safer, more digestible, and more palatable. If, when cooking plants, you find them bitter, change the water frequently until the bitterness disappears.

WHERE TO LOOK FOR WILD PLANT FOOD

Marshes, swamps, riverbanks, mud flats, inland water holes, margins of forests, shores of ponds and lakes, natural meadows, and protected mountain slopes head the list for good places to find food.

POOR HUNTING GROUNDS

Poor hunting grounds include high mountaintops, dense continuous forest stands, dry ridges, and desert areas. Do not waste your time hunting for food in these places. Head for better hunting grounds as fast as you can. Remember that water is your most important need, so watch for streams and springs as you search for food.

LEARN TO IDENTIFY EDIBLE PLANTS NOW

You will not need a degree in botany to identify enough wild edible plants to survive. Begin now to learn about plants before you face an emergency. Have someone point out a few plants to you. Go out on field trips frequently. Find a few plants and cook them to familiarize yourself with them. Learn to overcome any prejudices you may have in regard to eating unfamiliar foods. It is true, some of them will not taste as good as the cultivated foods you customarily eat.

EDIBILITY RULES

Never eat totally unfamiliar plants without first testing them to see if they are edible by preparing a cooked sample. Take a mouthful, chew it, and hold it in your mouth for five minutes. If at the end of this time it still tastes good, go ahead and eat it. However, if it tastes disagreeable, such as a bitter or nauseating taste, or a burning sensation, do not eat it. Spit it out. This signals danger. Do not take chances. The U.S. Air Force follows this edibility rule.

However, do NOT apply this edibility test to mushrooms. If you are not perfectly familiar with mushrooms, leave them alone.

Cook all plants when in doubt as to their edibility, for cooking frequently removes poisons. Of course, I must repeat, this does NOT apply to mushrooms. Also avoid eating untested plants that contain milky juice.

ADVANTAGES OF WILD FOODS

Nature supplies fresh, safe food in abundance, untouched by poisonous sprays. These wild foods are not handled by dirty pickers, nor by processors and salespeople, nor do hordes of customers pick them over, as you experience when shopping in supermarkets. They are not stored or transported over hundreds of miles to lose their vitamin and mineral content but are fresh and free for the picking. In becoming familiar with wild edible plants, you may add to your food supply at home a tasty variety of vitamin-packed foods!

Some feel that they can safely eat foods which birds or animals eat. In general, this is true. Food eaten by rodents, such as mice, rats, rabbits, and squirrels, or by other vegetable-eating animals will usually be safe for you to eat.

KEEPING FOOD COOL AND SAFE

You can keep foods cool in water from a stream or lake if you place them in waterproof containers. Indians long used cooling by evaporation. Join two containers (you may use buckets or large tin cans) with rope, with enough space between them to put food into the lower receptacle. Place water in the top vessel, filling it about two thirds full. If you have cheesecloth or loosely woven material such as burlap, weight it down in the center of the top vessel and let it down over the sides of the two containers, tying it about three inches below the lower vessel. The loosely woven material will absorb water from the top receptacle, and will drip on down, resulting in evaporation, which will cool the food in the lower container.

You can make a cooler by lashing limbs together, forming a frame. Make one shelf in the middle. Surround the frame with loosely woven material. Place a vessel of water on top of the frame. Place strips of the same material in the water, letting them hang down the sides of the framework. The strips will act as wicks, drawing water from the vessel, wetting the porous material which surrounds the sides of the frame. Evaporation will cool the cupboard, and the food will stay fresh a surprisingly long time. Hang this cooler on a branch in the shade.

If animals live in the area, suspend your food high enough to keep it out of reach. Make a safe cache by lashing two poles together at right angles in the form of a cross, and hang them from a limb. Balance the food tied to each end by equalizing the weight on each pole.

If you are in a very primitive area, dig a hole in a shady place, preferably under a tree. Line it with rocks, gravel, leaves, or grass. Place your food in this prepared pit, and cover the top and sides with dampened leaves or grass. Keep it damp by wetting it down frequently. This will keep your food cool and fresh for some time.

CHAPTER 4

EDIBLE SHOOTS
AND LEAVES—POTHERBS

It would be impossible to describe all of the potherbs in the United States, but we shall discuss some of the more commonly found edible shoots and leaves.

ASPARAGUS (*Asparagus officinalis*) p. 88*

Wild asparagus abounds in some areas but is fairly scarce in others. Birds have scattered the seeds from domestic plants. In the Eastern states, Middle West, and irrigated places in the West you can find this delicious plant, especially along fences, by the roadside, and in shaded areas. The tender young tips taste just as delicious as the kind you grow in your garden. Become familiar with the old dry stalk. When you spot the dead asparagus stalks, note the location and return later in the spring or early summer. When the weather begins to warm up, harvest the tender spears. Eat them in many ways: boiled and buttered, asparagus soup, creamed asparagus, or asparagus on toast.

BURDOCK—COMMON AND GREAT
(*Arctium minus, Lappa*) p. 88

Burdock, found all over the United States, is a member of the thistle family and grows along roads, fences, in vacant lots, around barns and stables, and, in fact, almost anywhere. It varies from two to six feet high and has large leaves shaped something like hearts. Peel the large tender leafstalks, and eat them either raw in

---

* Indicates page on which illustration is found.

29

a salad or cooked like asparagus. The root can also be eaten if obtained the first year. Peel and slice it, and cook it about twenty minutes. Drain, add fresh boiling water, and cook until tender. Serve it with butter or as you would parsnips.

Boil the leaves in at least two changes of water, but make sure they are young and tender. The young leaf-stalks may be added to homemade soup. The second-year rapidly growing flower stalk may be eaten just before the blossom matures. Peel the stalk carefully, seeing that you remove the strong, bitter skin. Cook the remaining succulent part in at least two changes of water, and serve with butter and salt.

CHICKWEED (*Stellaria media; Alsine media*) p. 88

Chickweed is a delicate little plant with tiny leaves and tiny white flowers. It grows all over the United States in gardens, fields, woods, or anywhere it can find a cool, moist place. You can find it almost the year round. Boil it like spinach, but use only the top stems and leaves. It tastes rather bland, so you may want to use it with other more strongly flavored greens, such as the dandelion, watercress, or mustard. Prepare and serve as you would spinach.

CHICORY (*Cichorium intybus*) p. 88

Chicory grows in the United States from Minnesota to Florida, in some of the Midwestern states, in the Southern states, and along the Pacific Coast. You will find it growing along roadsides. Recognize it mostly by its beautiful blue flowers, which may grow either singly or in clusters.

In the spring gather the tender young leaves and boil them in two or three changes of water, since they tend to be bitter. Serve as you would spinach. Indians have eaten the roots, but they are not the most tasty. If eaten, peel off the tough rind from the first-year roots, cut crosswise, and cook like parsnips until tender.

The root may also be used as a hot drink. Roast it until hard and brittle. Grind it into a fine powder, and prepare it as you would coffee or Postum. Since it is quite strong, experiment, using a small quantity at first.

CLOVER (*Trifolium pratense*) p. 88

Indians of the West, and probably elsewhere, have long eaten the red clover, along with other species, in salads. Gather the blossoms, and dry them (not in the sun) at room temperature. This preserves their flavor for making them into a tea. If you do not care for the flavor of the tea, mix it with fresh mint, which will enhance the flavor greatly.

CORN SALAD (*Valerianella locusta*) p. 89

You can eat this plant raw in salad, or cook it and serve it like spinach.

DANDELION (*Taraxacum officinale*) p. 89

Almost everyone recognizes this common plant—especially those who have to weed it out of their lawns! However, dandelions found in shady, lush grassy places taste much better. The roots are edible if peeled, sliced crosswise, and boiled in at least two changes of water. Serve as you would parsnips. The root can make a hot beverage very similar to that made from chicory roots. Roast until they snap and are dark brown (about four hours). Grind into fine powder, and brew as you would coffee or Postum.

The stems, just as they join the root, are white, or blanched, because they extend below the surface of the ground. Cut them off close to the root, and slice up to where the stem begins to turn green. Wash carefully to remove the grit, and boil as you would any vegetable, or else use them raw in a salad.

Gather the rosette of leaves, the best-known edible part of the dandelion, early while it is tender. Place in boiling water, and cook for about five minutes. Drain, and serve as spinach. Inside the white crown is the developing yellow blossom. Cut it out, and cook it for about three minutes. Drain, and season with butter or margarine. It *must* be in the embryonic stage, for it does not taste as good after the blossom begins to mature.

DOCK (*Rumex crispus*) p. 89

All of the many species of dock are edible. It grows along roadsides, in waste places, pastures, and cultivated fields; and nearly everyone recognizes it when it begins to go to seed. You may even find it in your own backyard! Gather the leaves when they are young and tender, especially in early spring. Since they are inclined to be a little bitter, boil them in two or three changes of water until the bitterness disappears. Some like to mix dock with other greens. It makes a valuable addition to your wilderness food supply, since it abounds in the spring.

FERNS (*Pteridium aquilinum*) p. 89

All fern fiddleheads are edible and abound all over the United States. Besides the fronds (fiddleheads), the tender stalks are also edible. Gather only the tender young stalks. Snap them off with your fingers as you would asparagus. Place the stalks, cut in two-inch lengths, in water, and boil until tender. Season with salt and margarine. To prepare the fiddleheads, place them in cold water, swish them around to remove the fine hairs, then pour off the water carefully. Add more cold water, and boil until tender. Serve as you would asparagus. You will be surprised at what a delicious dish this makes. Also, you can use the fronds raw in salads if they are very tender and young.

FIREWEED (*Chamaenerion angustifolium,* or *Epilobium angustifolium*) p. 89

Fireweed grows across the North American continent and is very common in burned-over land, hence its name. The flower ranges from pink to purple. Boil the tender leaves and young stalks as a potherb. The young shoots can be boiled also, as you would asparagus. Gather a quantity of the tender leaves. Melt margarine in a pan, add the fireweed leaves with a little water, salt slightly, and cover, simmering until just tender. Do not overcook. Serve immediately.

GREAT AMERICAN BULRUSH
(*Scirpus validus*) p. 90

This plant commonly grows in swamps all over North America. Indians of the Northwest reportedly ate the tender part of the base of the stem, fresh and raw.

HORSERADISH (*Radicula Armoracia*) p. 90

This plant is familiar from coast to coast. The leaf may grow as large as a foot long, and the root anywhere from six inches to a foot long and one to two inches in diameter. Some use the root in a sauce or powder. However, the tender young leaves in early spring may be boiled like spinach. Many mix them with other greens.

JEWELWEED, OR TOUCH-ME-NOT
(*Impatiens biflora*) p. 90

In the early spring or summer this succulent plant may be eaten. Boil the tender stems, and eat them as any vegetable.

LAMB'S-QUARTERS (*Chenopodium album*) p. 90

This delicious plant is ready to pick in the spring and summer. It grows all over the United States and may be gathered as late as early fall. Gather the young plants when they are less than a foot high. Boil about twenty minutes, and serve like spinach. They turn bitter when old, but if gathered correctly, they are not bitter at all. If the plant is mature, change the water at least twice. Gather the seeds, rub them between your hands to husk them, then grind them. You can mix them with regular flour, half and half, or add them to any pancake or muffin recipe for a "different" flavor.

MALLOW (*Malva rotundifolia*) p. 90

This beautiful plant, very common in gardens, along roadsides, and in pastures and wastelands, grows everywhere in America. Children enjoy eating the flat carpels, or "cheeses," which are good eaten raw. In some countries the people actually cultivate this lovely plant as a potherb. Pluck the tender round leaves, and boil as you would spinach, taking care not to overcook. Many regard the mallow as superior to conventional spinach.

MARSH MARIGOLD (*Caltha palustris*) p. 91

Marsh marigold, or cowslip, better known as a wild flower than as an edible plant, grows in swamps, in marshy places, or in any wet meadow, beginning to bloom in April or May, when bright-yellow flowers appear. Its marshy habitat makes it hard to get to, protecting it from people. The leaves and stems should be boiled like spinach and taste even better, according to some. Serve it creamed, or make it into a delicious soufflé. Use your spinach soufflé recipe, and be ready for a very pleasant surprise. It is very tasty. You must cook this plant before eating. It contains a poison which the boiling expels.

MEADOW BEAUTY (*Rhexia virginica*) p. 91

Also known as deer grass, meadow beauty usually grows in moist, sandy soil and has a sweet, yet acidulous, taste. Many gather this plant to put into salads to add zest and flavor. It is usually eaten raw.

MILKWEED
(*Asclepias syriaca; Gomphocarpus cordifolius*) p. 91

Few realize that the common milkweed is a very valuable wilderness food. However, do not think that any plant which has a milky juice is a milkweed. Positively identify your plant before you try to process it for eating. There are two well-known varieties: the purple milkweed (*Gomphocarpus cordifolius*) and the better-known common milkweed (*Asclepias syriaca*). Four or five parts of this plant are edible, but start all parts in *boiling* water—NOT COLD WATER—and change the water several times until the bitterness disappears. Add *boiling* water each time. If you start out with cold water, it will set the bitterness, and, no matter how many times you change the water, the bitterness will still remain.

The young plants from three to six inches high provide tender stalks which can be boiled as just described and taste somewhat like asparagus. Boil the tender young leaves in a similar manner. The unopened flower buds, just before the flower matures and while the buds are still in tight clusters, can be boiled in like manner, making a delectable dish. The young pods are delicious when prepared as described, but gather them at just the right stage—before the seedpod becomes tough and hard. Experience will teach you just the right time to pick them. Place them in a kettle of boiling water. Boil about a minute or two, drain, and add more boiling water. Repeat two or three times, or until the bitterness is removed. Then boil for about ten minutes until tender. They look like okra but taste different. You may season them as you would okra. Stewed tomatoes are good with them. After processing, you can freeze them for future use. Get acquainted with this plant *now*. The Indians also boiled and ate the roots.

MINER'S LETTUCE (*Montia perfoliata*) p. 91

An attractive plant bearing delicate white or pale pink flowers, miner's lettuce grows nearly everywhere and is well known as a salad plant. The leaves form a cup through which the stalk continues to grow. If very young and tender, use the leaves raw in salads. The leaves can also be boiled as a tender potherb. The Indians made a slightly laxative tea of the plant, using the stems as well as the leaves. Some claim that miner's lettuce will prevent scurvy.

MUSTARD (*Brassica nigra*) p. 91

Mustard hardly needs an introduction. However, everyone does not know how many parts of this plant are edible. Nearly everyone has enjoyed mustard greens. Many have gone out to fields and gathered the leaves instead of buying them in the markets.

When you gather mustard leaves in the fields, be sure to take only tender leaves from young plants. If you do this, they will not be bitter. Boil them a good thirty minutes. Gather a large quantity, for they tend to shrink as they cook.

The yellow blossoms of the mustard plant are edible— raw or cooked. If you cook them, do not overcook. Three minutes is maximum time, else they mush up and become very unattractive to serve. When picking the blossoms, do not include any of the top leaves, as they are very bitter. The roots of the mustard plant are also edible and, when boiled, taste very much like turnips. The seeds can be gathered and ground, to be used medicinally as a mustard plaster. Mix them half and half with flour and moisten slightly, forming a paste.

PEPPERGRASS (*Lepidium virginicum*) p. 92

Peppergrass, a member of the mustard family that grows in wastelands, can serve as a garnish. It has a peppery flavor and may be cut up in salads or used in soups to give a zesty flavor, but don't use too much.

PIGWEED (*Amaranthus retroflexus*) p. 92

The common pigweed, which is such a nuisance in our gardens, is a very good potherb. It has a mild flavor and is better when seasoned a bit. Pick it when very young and tender. It can be obtained from early spring to late fall in some places. Indians harvested the beautiful shiny black seeds, ground them, and used the meal to make bread and gruel. You can greatly improve the taste of the meal by roasting the seeds before grinding.

PLANTAIN (*Plantago major*) p. 92

The broad-leaved plantain, common in almost all of the states, is a very delicious potherb. It is tender when picked early in the spring and can be used raw in salads or cooked as greens. The narrow-leaved plantain, also edible, must have the water changed to render it less bitter. The narrow-leaved plantain also requires longer boiling time than the broad-leaved plantain and is not as tasty, but it must not be overlooked as a survival food. The broad-leaved plantain is rich in vitamins A and C.

POKEWEED (*Phytolacca americana*) p. 92

This plant, which must be used in the very young stage, is delicious when picked as a young shoot or sprout. Boil it a few minutes, and drain. Boil again in fresh salted water for about half an hour, or until tender. Season with butter or margarine. Do NOT use the leaves of the mature plant. Some have become violently ill by placing mature leaves in the blender to use in a green drink. If you do use the leaves for greens, pick them when very young and tender, and cook as described above for the young shoots.

PRICKLY LETTUCE (*Lactuca virosa*) p. 92

Prickly lettuce is found from coast to coast. The tender young leaves make a wonderful addition to salads or may be boiled for greens. Some prefer this plant to spinach. Do not overcook, and use very little water when cooking. Gather the tender young leaves early in the spring. In some places it grows until early summer.

PURSLANE, OR PUSSLEY (*Portulaca oleracea*) p. 93

This succulent plant, found all over the United States, has been used as a potherb mostly but can also be used in salads and soups. Wash it well, because it tends to be gritty. It has a mildly acid flavor, which some people enjoy. It resembles okra a little in that it is slightly mucilaginous, making it good in soups. The whole plant—leaves, stems, and flowers—may be eaten. Cook for ten minutes in salted water. Season with margarine. Some have made a casserole dish, using boiled tips, beaten eggs, and bread crumbs, seasoned as you would your favorite casserole. Bake in a moderate oven until set.

RUSSIAN THISTLE (*Salsola kadi tenuifolia*) p. 93

Most people would never think of this prickly plant as food! It grows all over the United States. Pick the young, tender plants when they are only a few inches high, wash them carefully, and boil them in salted water until tender. Served with butter or creamed, they are surprisingly tasty.

SCARLET PIMPERNEL (*Anagallis arvensis*) p. 93

This plant, also known as poor man's weatherglass, is found in almost all parts of the United States. Some eat the leaves raw in salads. Others prefer to cook the leaves and serve as spinach.

SHEEP SORREL (*Rumex acetosella*) p. 93

Most people are well acquainted with oxalis, or "sour grass." Sheep sorrel has the same acid flavor, which most children and adults enjoy. Use this plant in salads, as a garnish, or just eat it raw as you find it. It does not have the cloverlike leaves as the oxalis has, but has a short, slender, pointed leaf. You eat the leaf of the sorrel and the stem of the oxalis.

SHEPHERD'S PURSE (*Capsella bursa-pastoris*) p. 93

Shepherd's purse is found all over the world in fields and waste places. It is rather peppery. Use it raw, or cook it like spinach. When blanched and used in a salad, some think it tastes somewhat like cabbage. Wash the leaves well, as they will probably be gritty. The leaves grow as a rosette close to the ground. Some of the leaves are smooth and some roughly toothed. It has been suggested that the leaves be torn, not cut, into bite-size pieces when used in a salad.

STINGING NETTLE (*Urtica dioica*) p. 94

One would never guess that stinging nettle could be used as a food! Although it should probably be gathered with gloves, the stinging property of the tender young leaves fast disappears when boiled. It makes a delicious dish when served and seasoned as you would any greens. It is very rich in vitamin C and will prevent scurvy. It grows in waste places and along roadsides and has been seen along rivers and ponds occasionally. Although not too abundant in nature, it appears often enough to include it with the rest of the edible potherbs. The whole plant may be eaten when only a few inches high, as it is very tender. Just beware of the leaves when picking, because they have a dense covering of stinging hairs.

SWEET ANISE (*Foeniculum vulgare*) p. 94

Sweet anise, also called sweet fennel, is a beautiful fernlike plant with a delicate, sweet odor. The Indians gathered the young shoots and boiled them for greens. They made a tea from the roots and chewed the leaves for a laxative.

THISTLE (*Carduus oxidentalis*) p. 94

Of the many varieties of thistle, some having a bright purple blossom, others a flashing, brilliant red blossom, most are edible. Look for a plant having a large succulent stem, as this is the edible part. Wearing gloves and using a sharp knife, peel the outer layer of the stem, leaving the inner core, which is appetizing and tender. It tastes much like celery when eaten raw.

TRILLIUM, OR WAKE-ROBIN
(*Trillium grandiflorum*) p. 94

Trillium is another plant better known as a wild flower than as a food. The tender young leaves were boiled and eaten as spinach by the Indians. However, use it only as an emergency food.

TRUE SOLOMON'S SEAL
(*Polygonatum biflorum*) p. 94

Eat this plant in early spring, and boil like any vegetable. Some have served it like asparagus. The Indians ate the starchy root also.

VIOLET (*Viola pedunculata, palmata*) p. 94

This lovely plant is also known as blue violet or Johnny-jump-up. Cook the leaves as greens. In the spring whole hillsides may be thick with these beautiful little plants. The leaves of the cultivated violet plant are also edible. The mucilaginous wild plant will thicken soup.

WATERCRESS
(*Nasturtium officinale, aquaticum*) p. 95

Many do not realize that this plant may be boiled, seasoned, and served like any greens. Gather the leaves above the surface of the water. Also be sure the water is not contaminated if you plan to use the leaves raw in salads. If cooked, mix the leaves of watercress with other bland wild greens to enhance the flavor.

WILD CUCUMBER
(*Streptopus amplexifolius*) p. 95

Wild cucumber grows from Alaska to California and east to the Atlantic. The leaves are three or four inches long and about an inch wide, broad in the middle, and pointed at both ends. Do not confuse this plant with chilicothe (wild cucumber), which is a trailing vine with grapelike leaves. The chilicothe is also called man-in-the-ground or bigroot because of its enormous bitter root.

The *Streptopus amplexifolius* plant is also known as liverberry and twisted-stalk. Gather the fresh young shoots, and mix them with a salad, thus giving a cucumberlike taste. This is very welcome when you are in a wilderness area. Use the berries of the plant sparingly for a cathartic. The tender young leaves may also be used in salads. Some have eaten the thick rootstalk.

CHAPTER 5

ROOTS, TUBERS, AND BULBS

We cannot subsist on shoots and leaves alone. We must have carbohydrates, or energy foods, consisting of starches and sugars. Starch is found in roots, tubers, and bulbs. Sugar is found mainly in fruits. Shoots and leaves are somewhat seasonal, being more abundant in spring and summer. But roots, tubers, and bulbs may be found nearly all year round.

ARROWHEAD, OR WAPATOO
(*Sagittaria latifolia*) p. 95

This beautiful plant is found from coast to coast along streams, ponds, and in swampy, wet places. Its broad, pointed leaf, looking like a swallowtail, gives it the name of arrowhead. Remember, however, that all species do not have the distinct arrowhead-shaped leaf. Some have a rounded contour rather than the swallowtail at the bottom of the leaf.

All twenty species are edible. The tubers are starchy, and vary in size from BB shot, or peas, to a hen's egg. Most of them are about an inch in diameter. They are difficult to obtain, especially if the plant is located in a deep pond or ditch. The water is usually cold, and to stay in it for an hour or two digging out these tubers is very uncomfortable. The Indian women waded in and dug them out with their toes. When the tubers floated to the top of the pond, the Indians picked them up and placed them in their canoes. Some survivalists suggest donning hip boots and taking a rake, hoe, or potato hook and raking back and forth to free the tubers.

41

Arrowhead tubers are better when cooked, for they tend to be a little bitter if eaten raw. Cooked, they have an individual taste of their own, but somewhat resemble potatoes. Cook them with their skins on, a little longer than potatoes. In parts of California they are also known as "tule potatoes." They can be baked, boiled, roasted, creamed, scalloped, or French-fried. They make a delicious "potato" salad when used according to your favorite recipe. Combined with fresh peas or green beans, they equal the flavor of new potatoes.

ARROWROOT, OR COONTIE
(*Zamia Floridana, pumila*) p. 95

This fernlike or palmlike plant grows mostly in Florida. It has a large starchy root, which has served as a staple food of the Seminole Indians, who make it into a flour. The Indians baked little cakes or patties from it.

BRODIAEA (*Brodiaea grandiflora*) p. 95

Few realize that at the base of the long, slender stem of this well-known beautiful wild flower lies a very delectable, edible bulb. Brodiaea grow abundantly in fields, and all species are edible. The showy clustered flowers may be blue, purple, yellow, or white. The small bulbs are loaded with starch and are very tasty. You can boil them or chop them up raw in salads. The bulbs grow rather deep, and many times the soil is hard, so you may have to use a pick. Pulling on the stem will only leave the bulb in the ground, and it is nearly impossible to recover the bulb once the stem disengages from it. Experience will teach the forager just how to get these elusive, delicious, nutritious bulbs. The boiled bulb resembles the Irish potato in taste. Dig them only as a last resort, in order to preserve this lovely wild flower.

CAMAS (*Quamasia quamash*) p. 96

This wild flower with dark blue blossoms grows about two feet high in grassy, wet meadows. Its cousin, the white camas, or death camas, is poisonous, so be sure you know of a certainty that you have the *blue* camas. The Indians used to tie the blue camas stalks in bundles while still in bloom so that in the wintertime, when the blossoms were gone, they could distinguish between the blue camas and the white. However, the bulbs are usually gathered in the spring and summer.

The bulb must be cooked well to make it palatable. It is very starchy, therefore highly nutritious. Most people boil them, but the Indians used the pit method. They dug a hole, lined it with stones, and built a fire within. When the stones were hot, they raked out the embers, lined the bottom with green leaves, such as wild grape leaves, and placed the camas bulbs on them. Then they covered the bulbs with more leaves and placed earth over the leaves. They left them there all day and all night. In the morning they removed the earth and leaves, and the camas bulbs were tender, delectable, and ready to eat.

CATTAIL (*Typha latifolia*) p. 96

The cattail needs no description. It grows in wet, marshy land from coast to coast and in many parts of the world. Most people do not realize that several parts of the cattail plant are edible. It is a very important survival food and can save a life. Starting at the top, let us begin with the green bloom spikes. These are encased in a husk similar to corn but have only one layer. This spike is just above the part we know as the cattail. Pick the spikes when green and hard, just before the husk begins to come off. Do not gather them when they begin to turn yellow and thicken with pollen. Cook in salted water the same day you gather them.

When cooked, eat them like corn on the cob. They have a thin, tough, wiry center or core. If you wish, you may scrape off the green part from the core after cooking and serve like any vegetable. If eaten on the spike, dip in melted butter or margarine. This food will be a taste surprise to many. Some say that cattail spikes taste somewhat like artichokes. They can be frozen either cooked or uncooked on the spike, or may be scraped from the spike after cooking, and packaged and frozen.

Cattail casserole is delicious. For your first exposure to this unusual dish, mix one cup of cooked scraped cattail spikes, one-half cup bread crumbs, one egg slightly beaten, one-half cup milk, one-fourth teaspoon salt, one teaspoon G. Washington's Seasoning and Broth or other seasoning of your choice. Place in a small oiled casserole, and bake in a moderate oven (350 degrees) for thirty minutes, or until set. You may serve with or without gravy.

When the spike begins to turn yellow and thicken, pollen forms, which you can easily collect in a plastic bag. Insert the spike in the bag, hold the end closed, and shake vigorously. Pull out the spike, and repeat until you have collected enough "flour" to serve your purpose. Some have gathered a pound or two in an hour. This would make a nice project for the whole family, as everyone can take part. It is better to put the yellow pollen flour through a sieve to strain out all the undesirable chaff. This will yield a beautiful powdery yellow flour. You will obtain best results by mixing the yellow pollen flour half and half with wheat flour. Biscuits, pancakes, bread, or anything else usually made with regular flour can be made with this mixture. The pollen flour gives the mixture a beautiful yellow color as well as added vitamin A and protein. Some have used the pollen flour alone with fairly good results. Indians have used this flour for years. Pollen forms on the spikes around June, July, and August. Be on the lookout, for the season is very short, and you must be there at the exact time.

Another part of the cattail that can be eaten in the spring is the young shoot. It can be yanked out, exposing the white base. Peel it, leaving a tender white inner portion, which you can cook like asparagus. Cut it into inch or two-inch lengths, and boil in salted water until tender. In gathering these shoots, take care to grasp the inner leaves and gently tug until they slip out. You will soon become expert in gathering these delicate shoots. Cook them the same day you gather them, for they will not hold over even one day.

The rootstalk has a very starchy white core when peeled. Place several fresh rootstalks in a large pan of cold water. Separate the fibers, scraping the starch from the fibers with your fingers. Squeeze out the fibers and remove from the vessel. Strain carefully. Let the water stand until the starch settles to the bottom. Pour off the water carefully, leaving the starch on the bottom of the vessel. Add more fresh cold water, stirring vigorously. Let the starch settle again. Do this until you have a clean, almost-white layer of wet flour. Pour off as much water as you can. This flour is now ready for use in the wet state, or you can dry it and store it in a clean jar indefinitely. Again, you may mix this flour half and half with wheat flour, or it can be used in its pure state. Use in your favorite recipes for pancakes, muffins, biscuits, or bread. Obtain the rootstalks in the fall and winter in their best state, but you may dig them the year round.

At the base of the new sprout, where it joins the rootstalk, you will find a bulblike core, which is loaded with starch. These vary in size from a half inch to an inch in diameter and may be boiled and eaten. In the spring the rootstalks have elongated sprouts which are long, white, and tapered. They are crisp and delicious either cooked or raw. Even the rootstalks themselves may be cooked when peeled, and the starchy substance chewed. You will have to discard the fiber. Always eat all products of the cattail the same day you pick them.

You can now readily understand why the Indians considered the cattail a very valuable survival food, since it grows in abundance and so many parts are edible.

CHUFA, OR NUT GRASS (*Cyperus esculentus*) p. 96

This perennial bears tubers from its rootstalk. The tubers, clustered around the base of the plant, are about the size of the garbanzo. They have a sweet, nutty flavor and are a favorite with many people. Eat them boiled, or make a "milk" drink from the raw tuber.

COW PARSNIP (*Heracleum lanatum*) p. 96

Gather the flower scapes when they are nearly full grown but before the blossoms have opened. The leafstalks can also be used. Peel the stems as you would rhubarb. After cutting them into short sections, cook by boiling, pouring off the first water. They take a long time to cook and should not be considered done until the little cylindrical pieces are tender and begin to fall apart. Add milk, butter, and salt. Serve as you would creamed carrots. Some Indians burn the basal portion of the stalk and use the ashes as a substitute for salt. In the Yellowstone Park area the Indians change the water while boiling the root and then eat it. Some people have erroneously supposed this plant to be poisonous. Cattle are exceptionally fond of it.

DAY LILY (*Hemerocallis fulva*) p. 96

Few people realize that this beautiful cultivated flower also grows wild along roadsides and abandoned fields and that several parts are edible. Boil the unopened flower buds for only a few minutes, and season like any vegetable. You can also dip them in a rich egg batter and fry them, or add them to soups or stews. Soaking will make the withered blooms soft and pliable, then use them the same as you would the fresh blooms. In the spring when the sprouting stalks appear, use the tender inner portion cooked or raw in salads. If cooked, boil only a few minutes in salted water, and season. Serve like asparagus.

Also delectable are the tubers clustered under the day lily. They are only about one-half inch in diameter and about an inch long. Wash or scrub them thoroughly, and boil in salted water until tender. Be sure they are crisp and not soft or spongy. Slip off the skins, and serve with butter. Some say they taste a little like corn on the cob. When eaten raw, they have a crisp, nutty flavor. Chop them fine, and use in salads.

GROUNDNUT (*Apios tuberosa*) p. 97

This member of the pea family has a twining vine which grows in thickets and damp places. The sweet-tasting tubers resemble our cultivated potato. The Pilgrims lived on groundnuts their first winter. Indians used them as we use Irish potatoes. They are an excellent food whether boiled or roasted.

INDIAN CUCUMBER (*Medeola virginiana*) p. 97

Do not confuse this plant with wild cucumber (*Micrampelis oregana*), which is not edible. The edible species has from three to eight greenish-yellow flowers with six petallike segments. Indian cucumber has a thick rootstalk which is white, tuberous, and brittle, grows in rich, damp woods, and resembles the cultivated cucumber in both taste and smell. The plants have a whorl of three leaves. Eat the root raw like the cultivated cucumber.

INDIAN SOAPROOT
(*Chlorogalum pomeridianum*) p. 97

This brushy-covered bulb is edible. It grows from four to eight inches long and from two to four inches in diameter. After pulling off the brown fibrous covering (Indians used this fiber for making whisk brooms), roast the bulb whole if it is very tender and not fibrous inside. If it is tender and white, it can also be sliced and cooked. If very fibrous, all is not lost. Scrape the soft white fleshy portion from the fibers, and boil. Pour the water off, as it will be quite soapy. Then add fresh salted water, and boil until tender. It smells somewhat like Irish potatoes when boiling. Serve with butter, or cream it.

JERUSALEM ARTICHOKE
(*Helianthus tuberosus*) p. 97

This plant, related to the sunflower, grows quite tall along roadsides, in fields, and in waste places. The tubers look like Irish potatoes but are somewhat knobby at times. Collect them in the fall and winter. They can be eaten in a variety of ways. They are good peeled and sliced thin in tossed salads, or peeled, oiled, and roasted in the oven. They can also be boiled and mashed like Irish potatoes but are somewhat watery when served this way. One survivalist suggested a casserole dish, using boiled artichokes, bread crumbs, eggs, and seasoning. This nutritious tuber is low in starch.

ONION, WILD (*Allium cernuum*) p. 97

All of the many varieties, or species, of the genus Allium are edible. Some are strong; some are mild. The buds, just before bursting into full bloom, are delicious in salads or added to soups or stews. The bulbs are very nice boiled or sliced in a tossed salad. This plant is found all over the United States.

POND LILY OR WATER LILY
(*Nymphaea polysepala*) p. 98

Water lilies are found all over the world the year round. Since they grow in water, it is rather difficult to obtain the root. However, it is highly nutritious and well worth going after. Some species are rather bitter and require long cooking (as long as two hours or more) to remove the bitterness. Other species require less cooking time. Peel the root, and slice it before boiling. The young seedpod is also edible. Slice it, and boil until tender. The seeds, although bitter, are very nourishing. Parch them, and rub into flour between stones.

POTATO VINE (Man-underground)
(*Ipomoea pandurata*) p. 98

This plant closely resembles the sweet potato and is found along roadsides and in wastelands. The bush morning glory (*Ipomoea leptophylla*) is also edible. The roots of both of these plants are very large, some weighing as much as fifteen to twenty pounds, and are hard to extract from the ground. The flavor leaves much to be desired, but they are edible. Do not neglect or forget them when stranded without food in the wilderness. Peel the root, cut it up, and boil it in salted water. Some roots have a slightly bitter taste. Slowly roasting the roots in ashes or coals until tender helps remove the bitterness. If very large, it is best to cut them in pieces before roasting.

PRAIRIE (WILD) TURNIP (*Psoralea esculenta*) p. 98

The root of this plant is starchy and glutinous. The Indians ate it raw sometimes, but generally boiled or roasted it in their campfires. Gather the roots in June or July. Since the tops break off early and roll like tumbleweeds, the roots must be gathered while you can still identify the plant. The roots may be dried and eaten later in the fall or winter months. After drying the root thoroughly, pound it into meal, store it, and use it later for food.

RICE ROOT (*Fritillaria lanceolata*) p. 98

The large bulbs of this plant, also known as checkered lily, are covered with plump white, ricelike scales. The North Coast Indians dug and boiled the roots for food. Except for a slightly bitter taste, they are tender, delicate, and can scarcely be told from genuine rice. Serve with cream or butter and sugar, or season as you would any vegetable.

SALSIFY, OR OYSTER PLANT
(*Tragopogon porrifolius*) p. 98

Salsify grows quite tall and may be identified by its beautiful purple blossoms and its huge white seedballs that look like giant dandelion seedballs. The yellow salsify (*Tragopogon pratensis*) is also edible. The roots are edible only when tender, and some roots are so tough that they are not edible at all. Scrape the roots, and boil in salted water until done. Season as you would the cultivated salsify. You can prepare a very delicious soup, using wild salsify roots, milk, and seasoning.

SEGO LILY, OR MARIPOSA LILY
(*Calochortus nuttallii*) p. 99

This beautiful lily with its many species grows on hillsides, creating a flash of color. Some are white, some yellow, some a beautiful pink. The leaf is thin, narrow, and grasslike. The bulbs are edible and full of starch. In order to preserve the flower, use this delicious bulb only as a last resort. They would soon be gone if everyone began digging them up. The raw bulbs may be sliced thin and placed in salads, or they may be boiled and seasoned like Irish potatoes. They are delicious when served with butter or creamed.

VALERIAN (*Valeriana edulis*) p. 99

This strong-smelling plant has a carrot-shaped root which is black on the outside and bright yellow inside. Bake the roots to remove the bitterness. When properly prepared and cooked, they become sweet and quite palatable. The plant has small yellowish-white flowers and grows on wet plains and prairies.

YAMPA, OR SQUAWROOT (*Carum gairdneri*) p. 99

The Northwestern Indians found this plant highly nutritious. It grows on hillsides, in meadows, and on the plains. The roots may grow singly or in clusters. Peel the root, and boil it in salted water until tender. Serve with butter. The Indians used to dry the roots, grind them into flour, and make cakes or patties to take with them on trips.

There are many, many more edible roots and tubers, but it is impossible to describe them all.

CHAPTER 6

ACORNS, BUCKEYE, AND NUTS

ACORNS (*Quercus species*) p. 99

Every outdoorsman no doubt has wanted to know how to prepare acorns so that they can be eaten. Acorns are a highly nutritious wild food. To the Indians they were, and still are, a staple food, as potatoes and rice are to us. In preparing acorns, the Indians first dried the acorns in the shells. Then they roasted them, hulled them, and ground them into coarse meal or flour, using their grinding stones. They also used the cold-water leaching method. After drying the acorns in the sun, they hulled them and ground them into a coarse meal. Then they placed the meal in a woven basket and set it in a slowly running creek for a few days to get the tannin out, thus rendering the meal sweet and ready for use. The white oak and valley oak acorns are especially well suited to this cold-water method.

The modern cold-water leaching process is as follows: Dry the acorns in the sun or a slow oven. Hull them, and grind the meats in a food grinder, using a coarse-grind disk if you want meal instead of flour. Take a forty-two-ounce juice can in which holes have been punched in the bottom. Line the can with several layers of cheese-cloth to serve as a filter. Pour in the meal, and fill the can to the brim with cold water. Punch holes on opposite sides at the top of the can, and make a bail, using soft wire. Hang over a faucet, and let the water run just enough to allow it to filter through the can, yet not enough to run over the top. Leave it on all night. If the tannin is not out completely by morning, you will have to repeat the process until the meal is no longer bitter. Acorns vary in bitterness, but the most bitter acorn can be rendered sweet. If out in the wilderness, set your receptacle in a creek as described in the foregoing paragraph.

Another home method is the much faster boiling method. After drying the fresh acorns in the shell, hull them, and boil them whole or coarsely ground, starting with boiling water. If you start with cold water and bring to a boil, you will set the bitterness! Change the water when it darkens to the color of tea. Pour boiling water on them, and continue this about two hours, or until all bitterness disappears. You will find the acorns will have a sweet, nutlike flavor. Grind the acorns immediately, if boiled whole, and place in sterilized jars. Cap, and place in a slow oven (200 to 250 degrees Fahrenheit) for one hour if you want to preserve them. Or you may dry the whole acorns after processing, then grind into coarse meal or flour. Place this substance in jars, and can as described above. The meal will keep indefinitely. If you need the meal immediately, use it while it is damp. Some recipes will be given in a later chapter. You can use either the fine meal or flour in making bread, muffins, griddle cakes, or soup. Some have used fine acorn meal in the place of nuts in entrée recipes.

I talked recently to an elderly Indian woman who had been raised in an Indian village. She recalled going out with her mother and grandmother to gather wild plants and gave me a detailed account of how they processed acorns. Although I have already related several methods, I will give you the method her village used.

In the fall during acorn-gathering season, the Indians staged a camp-out, which the young people—and especially the children—looked forward to as an exciting occasion. After gathering the acorns, they dried them in the hulls, or shells. However, if they wanted to use them right away, they hulled them, rubbed off the tough skin over the meats, then dried them whole.

Next, whether hulled before or after drying, they used a special basket with a hole in the bottom and flaps on both sides at the bottom, called a pounding basket. They placed this basket over a flat rock, called a pounding rock, placed their legs over the flaps to hold the basket secure, and pounded the acorns into either a fine meal or a flour. If they wanted to make a porridge, they pounded the acorns into flour and sifted it. (She did not tell me what they used to sift the flour.) Then they placed a clean cloth over another basket, sprinkled the flour over the cloth, and poured water over the flour. They continued pouring the water until the flour was sweet. They sometimes dried this sweetened flour and stored it for future use. If they wanted to use it immediately, they put a vessel on the fire till the water boiled. Then they added boiling water a little at a time to the acorn flour so that it would not lump, stirring all the time while it was cooking. They cooked the flour for ten to fifteen minutes, then set the porridge aside to cool and thicken. They ate this with meat, fish, or whatever else they had. The Indians called it soup while it was still hot and porridge when it was cold and thick. No doubt different tribes in different areas used many other methods.

Some acorns, being more bitter than others, require a different method of leaching than those which are already sweet. You will have to experiment a little, but you will find it a lot of fun.

BUCKEYE (*Aesculus californica*) p. 99

The buckeye grows profusely all over America. The California buckeye, the one I am the most familiar with, abounds all over California. The Indians had different ways of leaching buckeye, as they did with acorns. One of the most popular methods was the cold-water method, allowing a slow-running stream to flow through the meal, which they placed in a woven basket. It took several days but accomplished the job very well. When there was a bumper crop, they buried some in the ground and dug them up in the spring. By then the rains had leached them out so that they were nice and sweet. I have never tried this.

The Indians also boiled the buckeyes with the brown skin for ten to fifteen minutes, then peeled the brown skin off and sliced them like potatoes. They then placed them in a woven basket (or colander) and set it in a large pan of water (or the creek). If set in water, change the water every day for four days. Then they should be sweet and ready to use. Salt them, and use the same way you would potatoes.

Some Indians used the quick-boiling method if they were hungry and did not have much food to tide them over. You may want to try it yourself. Gather the buckeyes, hull them from the thick gray capsule, peel off the tough brown skin, and grind them into coarse meal. You could use a food grinder in your home. Place the meal in a vessel, and pour boiling water over the meal. Do not start with cold water and bring to a boil, for you will set the bitterness. Boil about ten minutes. Pour off the water, and pour more boiling water over the meal. Continue to cook another ten minutes. Repeat this process for about two to three hours, depending upon the bitterness of the buckeye. If you put this in a sieve, be careful not to press too hard or it will go right through the sieve and you will get very little meal. Just let it run through without pressing much. Taste the meal after about an hour or two. Do not taste the water you pour off, because it will be bitter to the end since it contains the tannic acid leached out of the buckeye. I will give a few recipes in another chapter, including cream of buckeye soup.

Remember that the buckeye abounds in the fall and is highly nutritious. If canned, buckeye meal will keep indefinitely.

BEECHNUT (*Fagus grandifolia*) p. 100

The beechnut is very small but both delicious and nutritious. Beechnuts grow in pairs in a small, bristly burr and mature in October. Eat them raw or cooked. These nuts abound in the northern states and Canada.

BLACK WALNUT (*Juglans nigra*) p. 100

The black walnut, found almost everywhere from coast to coast, may grow nearly one hundred feet tall, with a trunk nearly six feet in diameter. The hull makes an almost permanent stain when shucked from the nut. The nutmeats are rather difficult to extract but can be picked out in broken pieces quite readily. The trees are frequently found in the wilderness. However, the English walnut, which is usually grafted onto a black walnut tree, will usually be found on ranches or near civilization. Perhaps an old abandoned ranch will yield a walnut tree far from habitation.

BUTTERNUT (*Juglans cinerea*) p. 100

This fine nut tree grows from Canada down to Georgia and Mississippi and as far over as Kansas and Arkansas. It has also been found in Ohio. No doubt in other states this tree may be found growing in rich loamy soil. The nuts grow in clusters of two to five. The shell is hard and bony, but it is not hard to separate the kernel. Because the nut is quite oily, it should be stored in a cool place to prevent its becoming rancid. It is a sweet and delicious nut.

CHESTNUT, AMERICAN (*Castanea dentata*) p. 100

This tree, which sometimes grows to a height of one hundred feet, has a bristly, spiny burr containing from one to three brown, glossy, sweet-tasting nuts. Some people relish this nut, but many do not appreciate it because they do not know how to use it. The nuts ripen about October, and bushels of them can be gathered and stored for winter use. A later chapter will include a recipe or two which might inspire readers to explore a new taste thrill. Do not confuse American chestnut with horse chestnut (*Aesculus carnea* [red] or *A. hippocastanum* [common]), which is in the buckeye family and is not edible as far as I know.

CHINQUAPIN
(*Castanea pumila; Castanopsis chrysophylla*) p. 101

This tree varies in size from a bush, a tree thirty to forty feet high, to one hundred feet high as is the case of *Castanopsis chrysophylla*, which is found mostly in northern California and Oregon. The latter tree bears leaves similar to the American chestnut, and the nut is very sweet. They mature about September. The *Castanea pumila* is more of a shrub, with small spikelike clusters of burrs resembling the acorn in shape. The Indians favored the nuts from all chinquapin species.

HAZELNUT (*Corylus americana, rostrata*) p. 100

Hazelnuts grow from Maine to California. Sometimes the bracts grow singly and sometimes in pairs. I have seen three growing together many times. The hazelnut, rounded at the bottom, tapers to a tubelike beak or neck. The nut is found at the bottom of this enclosure. They grow profusely and of all nuts are most likely to be found in abundance in the wilderness. Gather them from August until late fall. Eat them raw or cooked, the latter especially in candy, cake, or nut entrée recipes.

HICKORY (*Carya ovata, glabra,* or *alba*) p. 100

This wonderful nut grows on a tree which may attain a height of one hundred feet or more. It has a thick four-valve husk. The small, sweet nut is enclosed in a thick, hard, bony shell. Most hickory trees grow in the East and Midwest. It is a real "find" to come across a hickory-nut tree in the wilderness. Remember, nuts are high in protein and fat, both of which are not too easy to find in the wilderness.

PINE NUT (*Pinus sabiniana,* Digger pine; or *Pinus edulis,* piñon) p. 101

All pine cones contain pine nuts. However, some of

the pine nuts are so small that it would be a real chore to harvest enough to make it worthwhile. The ponderosa pine is an example. The piñon pine nut is more than half an inch long and has little narrow wings attached. The Indians of Utah, Nevada, Arizona, and California still gather them. The nuts are sweet and very pleasant either raw or roasted. They are high in protein and fat. Pine nuts mature in autumn. The Digger pine nut is very large, with a hard shell. Cracked carefully, the nut can be obtained intact. Indians often roast them, pound or grind them into meal, and bake cakes or cook the meal as a gruel. A pack rat nest may contain as much as a quart of pine nuts, along with edible roots, etc.

It would be useless to mention the many other nuts found in the wilderness. I am sure that you are well acquainted with most nuts. Just remember that all nuts are a fine source of protein and fat (polyunsaturated fatty acids).

CHAPTER 7

WILD FRUITS

The wilderness yields a large variety of delicious wild fruits during the summer and autumn months, anywhere from June through October.

BLACKBERRIES
(*Rubus laciniatus, vitifolius, nigrobaccus*) p. 101

The numerous species of blackberries are probably the best known and the most easily identified of any of the wild berries. They contain much vitamin C and are available in abundance during the summer and autumn months. The berries are delicious fresh or cooked. You can also dry them for future use. The leaves make an excellent tea, and Indians used to chew on tender peeled sprouts and twigs.

BUNCHBERRIES (*Cornus canadensis*) p. 101

Bunchberries are bright red and taste rather insipid. You can make them into jam, fruit soup, or pudding. They ripen in the summer.

CHOKECHERRIES (*Prunus virginiana*) p. 102

This berry grows on a plant which may range anywhere from a shrub to a twenty-foot tree. The dark red fruit, about the size of a pea, is very sour and astringent. When cooked, however, this quality disappears somewhat. They make good jelly, but, because they lack pectin, you might mix them with crab apples when making jelly.

CRANBERRIES (*Viburnum opulus; vaccinium*) p. 101

The highbush cranberry (*opulus*) is a bright red berry hanging in clusters almost like grapes. The berry is sour and slightly bitter. Indians made jelly from them. When one is out in the wilderness and finds himself thirsty, the highbush cranberry is very welcome because it will quench the thirst better than most berries. They ripen around July and may be found through most of the winter months. The lowbush cranberry (*vaccinium*) grows low to the ground. The tart berries make good sauce with sugar added. If you see a bumper crop, gather lots of them, spread them out to dry either in the hot sun or in a hot room until they will mash to powder. Reconstitute them by placing them in water. Then boil them, add sugar, and you will have a tasty cranberry sauce. They can also be stored fresh if you gather them on a hot, dry day and place them in a cool cellar.

CURRANTS
(*Ribes vulgare, glandulosum, aureum*) p. 102

There are many species of currants, also. The golden currant, red currant, and fetid currant are commonly found in the wilderness. The sour fruit, a very valuable thirst quencher, is used mostly for making jelly.

DEWBERRIES (*Rubus procumbens*) p. 102

The dewberry vine trails along in the woods for several feet. The white flowers are an inch in diameter. It bears a large, nearly inch-long black berry. Although the plant grows abundantly, it does not have as large a production of berries as the blackberry. It enjoys a rocky or gravelly dry soil. It is a very welcome find in the wilderness. Eat it as you would any other berry.

ELDERBERRIES (*Sambucus canadensis, glauca*) p. 102

This beautiful shrub (*canadensis*) grows abundantly all over the United States. California Indians made the cream-colored blossoms into a delicate tea. They can also be mixed with batter and fried or baked into cakes. The berries are deep purple, very small, and thickly clustered. They have a mild flavor and can be eaten fresh but are best when used to make pies, jam, or jelly. The *glauca* species may grow to a height of forty feet. I have seen many trees as high or higher. The fruit is sweet and very juicy, making excellent pies.

GOOSEBERRIES
(*Ribes cynosbati, oxyacanthoides*) p. 102

The prickly gooseberry (*cynosbati*) is found from Maine to California. It grows so profusely in forest areas that people are hired to grub it out. The stems have spines near the base of each cluster of berries. The berries turn from green to brownish-red when ripe. Because of the prickles, eat them with care if you eat them fresh off the vine. They make excellent sauce, pie, jelly, and preserves. The smooth-fruited gooseberry (*oxyacanthoides*) has spines on the branches, but the fruit is smooth and turns reddish-purple when ripe. This plant grows in Canada and the northern United States. All gooseberries ripen in midsummer, July and August.

GRAPES (*Vitis californica, aestivalis*) p. 103

Many species of wild grapes grow from coast to coast. Eat the tender leaves as greens. The Indians wrapped food in grape leaves to bake over coals, covered with earth. Wild grapes are purple when ripe, and some species are quite sweet. Most of them, however, are rather tart and some are insipid, but they can be made into pies or jelly.

GROUND-CHERRIES (*Physalis pubescens*) no illus.

This pretty little plant grows from six inches to a foot high. The fruit, encased in a papery-thin husk, is golden yellow when fully ripe and quite pleasant to the taste. If stored in the husk in a cool place, it will keep for weeks. I am always delighted when I run across this delicious fruit. This plant is sometimes called strawberry tomato.

MANZANITA BERRIES
(*Arctostaphylos manzanita*) p. 103

There are dozens of species of manzanita. The berries range from brownish-red to bright red, and from as small as holly berries to the size of a large pea. The larger berry is sweeter and rather mealy and quite pleasant to the taste. All manzanita berries are slightly acid, tasting somewhat like green apples. Indians ate them ripe, right off the bush, or roasted them or made a pleasant drink from them. They also made them into jelly and dried and ground them into a meal to be used as a porridge. Manzanita berries rank next to acorns in food value.

MAYAPPLE (*Podophyllum peltatum*) p. 103

Some books list the mayapple as poisonous. Always eat it with caution. Some people have suffered severe colic after eating only two small mayapples the size of a hen's egg. The egg-shaped yellow fruit tastes somewhat like strawberries to some. It has numerous seeds and a tough skin. Some prefer to cook it into a sauce, adding sugar. Eat *sparingly!*

MULBERRIES (*Morus rubra, alba*) p. 103

I well remember how surprised I was when I saw and ate my first mulberry. I had no idea that any berry grew on a tree. Some trees attain a height of thirty to sixty feet. The fruit is considered rather insipid by some, while others thoroughly enjoy its unique flavor. The berries are bright red and long—some an inch and a half long. They are delicious eaten with sugar and cream. They can also be made into pies and jam. Make a delicious drink by placing them in a blender. You may want to add a little sugar and lemon juice.

OREGON GRAPES (*Berberis aquifolium*) p. 103

This plant is found from the Rocky Mountains to the Pacific Coast. The dark blue berries form in clusters and ripen in autumn. They somewhat resemble cultivated grapes and can be made into a beverage, eaten fresh, or made into jelly.

PASSIONFLOWER (*Passiflora incarnata, lutea*) p. 104

This beautiful plant bears a large white blossom about two inches in diameter. It has a crown of purple or pink threadlike filaments. The yellow fruit is the size and shape of a hen's egg. Some call it maypop. It is gathered from August to October and makes what some consider a very refreshing drink. The fruit can be eaten fresh or cooked. The *lutea* has a bright yellow flower and a purple fruit which may be either round or oblong. The juice is purplish in color. The fruit of the *lutea* is smaller, growing from a half to three quarters of an inch in diameter. They can be made into a pleasant beverage or jelly.

PRICKLY PEAR (*Opuntia vulgaris, humifusa*) p. 104

Again, there are numerous species of cactus fruits. The plants are found on rocky or sandy soil. Some grow near the coast, others in desert areas. To a hungry and thirsty traveler, the cactus has been a lifesaver. Be careful in handling them, because they have vicious spines and annoying bristles on the fruit itself. These bristles are so small that they are almost invisible. Even if you cannot see them, remember that they are there—as you will soon discover if you do not wear plastic or leather gloves. After removing the bristles, eat the fruit fresh, or cook it, or, if you prefer, can it for future use.

The pears are small, usually from one-half to two inches long. The new, tender joints can be peeled and boiled, or fried either plain or with batter. They are succulent and juicy and quite mucilaginous. The Indians used them over sores or ulcerations as a poultice. My brother had a time with a broken blister on his heel when he was a child. Red streaks appeared, and my mother grew worried. Her brother-in-law had heard of an old Indian remedy, and they decided to try it. He found a cactus leaf, split it, and cut a small portion to fit over the heel. They bandaged it on and left it overnight. In the morning they took it off. The cactus was brownish-black, and my brother's heel was white and wrinkled like a dried prune, but it healed up right away. Now, I am not prescribing, just reciting a personal experience. What worked for my brother over forty years ago may not work for anyone else.

PYRACANTHA BERRIES
(*Pyracantha graberi, coccinea*) p. 104

I was surprised to find that there are so many kinds of pyracantha, all of which are edible. Some form stiff shrubs, used as hedges; others are creeping types. Some bear red berries, some orange, others variegated. It is best known as a cultivated plant, but one may come across a bush on an abandoned ranch or an out-of-the-way homestead. Many are surprised to find that the berries are edible, for they had assumed that they were poisonous. They are not. I have eaten them for years. Eat the berries fresh off the bush or make them into delicious pies. The robins like these berries also, so you will have to hurry to get there first!

RASPBERRIES
(*Rubus strigosus, occidentalis, leucodermis*) p. 104

Of the numerous species of raspberries, some black, some red, all are edible. It is a genuine pleasure to run across wild raspberries on hikes or camping trips. They are plentiful and grow wild in low elevations and higher elevations up to four thousand feet. The sticky stems and leaves are whitish-green and downy in appearance. Birds, bears, and other animals are very fond of the sweet, luscious berries. They can be eaten fresh or made into jam or jelly. They can also be dried. Some enjoy raspberry pie. When served fresh with sugar and cream, what could be more delectable?

SALMONBERRIES (*Rubus spectabilis*) p. 104

It is difficult to differentiate between some of the raspberries, thimbleberries, dewberries, and salmonberries. I do not attempt to be an expert. Even botanists have difficulty. I *do* know that the salmonberries I have seen have a beautiful white blossom and a purple berry which looks very much like a raspberry. The leaves are not quite as bristly as the raspberry's. The salmonberry is delicious and can be eaten the same as other berries.

SERVICEBERRIES (*Amelanchier canadensis*) p. 104

This berry, also known as Juneberry or shadbush, grows on a tree to a height of from six to fifty feet. The tree has a light-colored smooth bark and bears red or purplish berries which grow in clusters. The berry may also grow on short bushes. They are sweet and can be eaten fresh or made into pies. They can also be dried or canned for future use. This is an excellent berry.

STRAWBERRIES
(*Fragaria virginiana, vesca, chiloensis*) p. 105

This beautiful little plant needs no description. Even children recognize this berry anywhere. The strawberry grows along streams, on the edge of wooded areas, in fields—in fact, almost anywhere. Certain species grow on sand dunes and on beaches. The berries are usually red, but I have seen and eaten white berries, growing wild, which were very sweet and delicious. Some feel that wild strawberries are more desirable than cultivated ones, although some varieties are rather insipid. Regardless of flavor, this is an important berry to find in the wilderness.

THIMBLEBERRIES
(*Rubus argutus, parviflorus*) p. 105

The thimbleberry plant is beautiful, the leaves attracting as much attention as the lovely white flower or the scarlet berry. The leaves are circular—three ovate leaflets with unequal serrations. The fruit looks very much like a raspberry. The plant likes shade and grows in elevations from 1,500 to 7,000 feet. The highbush thimbleberry grows from three to nine feet high, while the shorter varieties range from one to three feet. The highbush thimbleberry has a black fruit ranging from a half inch to an inch long. The shorter varieties have a much smaller scarlet berry. I have seen them growing so thick along the redwood highway in Humboldt County, California, that they made a hedge stretching for miles. The fruit was so abundant that it created a gorgeous intermingling of red and green. The thimbleberry has been found in Michigan, New Mexico, and Alaska, so I presume it may be found almost anywhere.

TOYON BERRIES
(Photinia arbutifolia; Heteromeles arbutifolia) p. 105

Toyon berries are also known as California holly berries or Christmas berries. Everyone knows this berry as the decorative berry used in making wreaths, etc. Few realize that the Indians have eaten these berries for years. They abound on the hillsides, maturing from October through January. The Indians made a tea from them or ate them raw or roasted. They also dried them, then parched them and made them into a meal. Some boiled or baked them. They are highly nutritious. Although they are not as tasty as some berries, do not neglect them when food is scarce in the wintertime.

TWINBERRIES *(Mitchella repens)* p. 105

Twinberries, also known as partridgeberries, grow on a trailing vine, with glossy, rather heart-shaped leaves. The flowers are either white or pink. The scarlet berries appear to be two berries united at the base. They are not too abundant but are very tasty and slightly aromatic. If you once see this berry, you will not quickly forget it. Eat it fresh or cooked.

So many fruits grow in the wilderness that it is impossible to enumerate or describe them all. No doubt you are thinking right now that I have not mentioned your favorite wilderness fruit! Every locale will have its own native varieties. Field trips will yield many exciting experiences as you discover new wild fruits. On your outings, keep wild plants in mind. You will be richly rewarded.

Chapter 8

PLANTS USED FOR GARNISHES AND SEASONINGS

IRISH MOSS (*Chondrus crispus*) p. 105

This seaweed or alga-type plant grows near the seashore, clinging to rocks and sometimes growing underwater. Ranging from two or three inches to a foot long, it varies anywhere from a green to a brown. It is usually dried for future use and bleaches out when drying. This dried moss is placed in soups to thicken them; and, according to Medsger, it can be made into jelly, custard, pudding, etc. It contains starch as well as iodine and is valuable nutritionwise when one is on the coast.

ICELAND MOSS (*Cetraria islandica*) no illus.

This plant is really not a true moss, but a lichen. It grows not only on rocks, but on the ground. It is a very low, small plant, usually growing not higher than three or four inches and is brown or grayish-brown. When dried, it also loses some of its color. It is quite bitter, but boiling removes much of this. After removing the bitterness, dry it, and make it into a flourlike consistency by rolling on a hard surface. In years past Indians used it to make bread or cakes. It is high in sugar and starch, thus highly nutritional.

LOCUST (*Robinia pseudoacacia; Gleditsia triacanthos; Ceratonia siliqua*) p. 106

The locust tree grows everywhere I have ever been. The Robinia is best known for its seeds. The pods are two or three inches long, bearing small seeds which are oily and slightly acid-tasting when raw. The Indians boiled these seeds as we boil beans. When cooked, the seeds lose their acid flavor and are quite tasty if seasoned with tomatoes, onions, and a little sweet bell pepper. The Gleditsia, or honey locust, is slightly taller than the Robinia, growing to nearly one hundred feet. It is best known for its long pods—ten to fifteen inches. The pods are thin, flat, yet slightly curved. A fleshy, sweet pulp between the seeds is rather pleasant to chew on. The Ceratonia is probably the best known of the three varieties of locust. Its pod grows to be about eight or ten inches long and is thick and fleshy, almost moist. The sweet pulp between the seeds is chewy and very pleasant and is known as Saint-John's-bread. You can buy carob powder in health-food stores. This is dried, powdered locust pod pulp and is used in place of chocolate. You can make your own, so why not experiment with it?

ROSE HIPS (*Rosa californica, pisocarpa,* etc.) p. 106

There are so many species of wild roses that it would take a whole page just to list a portion of them. However, since most people are very familiar with this beautiful stickery plant, it needs no description. Most people do not know that the seedpod, known as the rose hip, is edible. The rose hip is high in vitamin C, iron, calcium, and phosphorus. Three rose hips fresh from the wild rosebush equal an orange in vitamin C.

To eat fresh, cut the rose hip in two and remove the seeds. Most fleshy, orange-colored rose hips have the taste of fresh apples, but some are strong flavored. Cut up rose hips in salads, or make them into jam, jelly, or syrup. To make the syrup, collect about a half kettle of rose hips, cover with water, and boil gently. When soft, pour the juice through a strainer. Save the juice. Return the pulp to the kettle, cover with water, and boil again. Add one cup of sugar to two cups of juice, and boil until thick. Can in jars to preserve for future use.

MESQUITE (*Prosopis glandulosa*) p. 106

This shrub or small tree grows in dry soil and on deserts. It has been found in Texas, New Mexico, Arizona, California, and from Kansas to Nevada. It probably grows in any state where it can get dry soil and weather. The root goes down from thirty to sixty feet searching for water. The bush has bean-shaped pods ranging from three to six inches in length. Indians used this pod for a sugar substitute because the pulp between the seeds in the pod is very sweet. They ate the pods when green, cooked as a vegetable, as well as the ripened pod. They also dried the pods and made them into meal, from which they baked bread or cakes. The meal is highly nutritious.

SCREW BEAN (*Prosopis pubescens*) p. 106

This shrub or small tree looks very similar to mesquite except the leaves have only five to eight pairs of leaflets while the mesquite has numerous narrow leaflets. The pods of the screw bean are shorter and twist like a corkscrew. The pulp in the pod is very sweet, much like the mesquite. The Indians dried the pods and made meal from which they baked little cakes to take on hunting trips or when moving from place to place. They also made a syrup from the pods. Some Indian tribes made a drink from the pods by boiling them.

TARWEED (*Madia sativa, elegans, robusta*) p. 106

This common weed bears a yellow flower. The Indians used the seeds for various things. They expressed oil from the seeds for frying or to use as a dressing for salads. They also used this oil as a lubricant. They boiled the seeds, which produced an oil which they used in making soap. Some tribes ground the dry seeds into a meal (pinole), which they ate with relish or baked into cakes. Sometimes they mixed other things such as acorn meal or other seed meal with ground tarweed seeds in making their meal or pinole. Remember that all seeds contain oil, which is hard to find in the wilderness.

LUPINE
(*Lupinus perennis, andersonii, laxiflorus,* etc.) p. 107

It would take a whole chapter just to enumerate and describe the different varieties of lupine. In general, however, most lupine seeds are edible. I have never tried any that were not. The seeds are usually bitter until boiled. You may have to change the water once or twice to remove this bitterness. Indians cooked them like our domestic peas. Some tribes steamed the leaves and flowers early in the spring when tender or boiled them like greens. Sometimes they ate the leaves and flowers with their acorn soup.

VETCH
(*Vicia sativa, exigua, americana, gigantea*) p. 107

There are several varieties of vetch. The species with which I am personally acquainted is *exigua,* commonly known as California vetch. The pods are gathered when green and tender and cooked whole like string beans. They taste good and are highly nutritious. Some wait until the seeds ripen, hull them, and cook them like cultivated peas. The seeds are very starchy.

WILLOW
(*Salix lasiandra, laevigigata, argophylla,* etc.) p. 107

There are over three hundred species of willow in all the world. This tree needs no description, I am sure. Eat the inner bark only as a last-resort emergency food. The young shoots can be eaten after removing the outer bark. The leaves have been found to be high in vitamin C. Some Indians, when food was very scarce, cut the inner willow bark, ground it into flour, and used it to make cakes and porridge. Some willow species are quite bitter, while others are fairly sweet and palatable.

YUCCA (*Yucca baccata, glauca*) p. 107

This desert plant is an important one for those who find themselves stranded in dry, desert areas. Various Indian tribes gathered the flowers and boiled them. They chewed the stalk for its sugar content. The fruit is large and pulpy and cherished by the Indians. They ate it fresh, cooked, or roasted. It can also be dried and stored for future use. The root was crushed and used for shampooing the hair or washing clothes.

Chapter 9

PLANTS USED FOR BEVERAGES

Since most teas are prepared the same way, I will list several that may be made from plants found in the wilderness and spend some time describing the more interesting varieties or those requiring special preparation. Leaves, flowers, twigs, bark, and roots are all used to make beverages in the wilderness.

CHICORY (*Cichorium intybus*) p. 88

The most commonly known and used coffee substitute is the chicory root. After gathering the root, thoroughly wash it and dry it until it becomes quite brittle. Then grind it to the same consistency as the coffee bean, and brew exactly the same as coffee. Experiment with it until you get a nice, not-too-bitter or strong flavor.

DANDELION (*Taraxacum officinale*) p. 89

Another widely used coffee substitute is the dandelion root. Like the chicory, the roots are gathered, washed, and dried until brittle, then ground and brewed like coffee. However, dandelion root has a tendency to be strong, so use much less grounds than chicory to avoid getting a strong, bitter taste.

SPICEBUSH (*Benzoin aestivale*) p. 107

This fragrant, beautiful bush has been used for tea for centuries. The leaves, twigs, and bark are all used. After placing in water, boil for fifteen to twenty minutes. Strain, and drink with sugar and milk the same as you would cultivated tea. Some think that this bush has a stimulant in it, for many a tired and weary traveler has felt invigorated after drinking a refreshing cup of spice-bush tea.

SASSAFRAS (*Sassafras variifolium*) p. 108

This tree, well known to Easterners, has been found in Michigan, the New England states, Florida, Iowa, and Kansas. No doubt it grows in other states or in any place where it can find dry, sandy soil. It has a greenish-yellow blossom. The bark of young roots is used to make the tea. When boiled, the tea becomes red. Serve it like tea, with cream and sugar.

SWEET BIRCH (*Betula lenta*) p. 108

The birch tree is noted for its beautiful white bark, which the Indians used in many ways. However, a tasty tea may be made by cutting up small, tender twigs and boiling them in birch sap for a few minutes. Add cream and sugar, and a very wholesome and delicious tea results. To get the birch sap, tap the birch tree as you would a maple tree, by boring a hole about three inches deep in the trunk of the tree about three feet above the ground. Hammer a spile into the hole, or make your own by obtaining a stiff four-inch-long twig, hollowing it out, and notching it at one end to hang a small bucket or pail to collect the sap. Most birch trees will yield all the sap you will want to use in just a few hours.

You can drink the sap right out of your pail if you wish. It has the taste of pure water with a very slight suggestion of wintergreen flavor. Birch tea can also be made from the inner bark of the root or stump of the tree. Cut in small pieces and *steep* in boiling water, but do not boil. You can also mix pieces of tender birch twigs with pieces of inner bark to make a nice, rather strongly wintergreen-flavored tea. To make a still stronger tea, add young birch leaves to the twigs and bark.

PERSIMMON
(*Diospyros Kaki, lotus, virginiana*) p. 108

The leaves of the persimmon tree are high in vitamin C. A pleasing tea can be made from the fresh leaves, but some people prefer the tea made from the dried leaves. Steep the same as any commercial tea.

CLOVER (*Trifolium pratense*) p. 88

Many are well acquainted with clover tea. Gather the blossoms, and dry them gradually at room temperature—never in the sun or in the oven. Steep like any tea.

MINT
(*Mentha piperita, viridis, spicata, canadensis*) p. 108

Mint grows everywhere, especially near streams or water of any kind. It usually has a fragrance which immediately identifies it, but if you are not sure it is mint, crush the leaves and you will have no further question, for its fragrance will fill the air. Most people make their tea from the dried leaves, but personally I much prefer fresh mint tea. Just go out in the woods, pick a few dozen leaves, bring them home, pour boiling water over them, and steep for a few minutes. This tea has a delicious flavor. *Piperita* is peppermint, and *spicata* or *viridis* is spearmint. Oil is distilled from spearmint to flavor gum and candies. Peppermint oil and oil of wintergreen are used medicinally. *Canadensis,* an American wild mint, is found from coast to coast.

SUMAC (*Rhus typhina, glabra*) p. 108

This beautiful shrub or small tree bears large red clusters of berries, which are covered with tiny little hairs. Gather these fruit clusters, and place in cold water. Crush the berries, tearing them off the sticky and stickery stems. Let stand in cold water a few minutes, then strain. The results? A pleasant, slightly acid drink. Indians used it in summertime much as we use lemonade. In fact, it is known as Indian lemonade.

Do not make the mistake of boiling the water in order to get a stronger flavored drink which you think you might dilute, thus making more of the drink. It does not work. It ruins the delicate flavor and becomes bitter and very unpleasant. You do not have to set the berries in cold water long. In a very few minutes you will have the desired delicate, sour flavor.

NEW JERSEY TEA (*Ceanothus americanus*) p. 109

The New Jersey tea shrub dies each winter but sprouts in the spring. Its blossoms are white and form in clusters. The leaves are from two to three inches long, alternate, and ovate. Pick the leaves when the blossoms are still on the shrub. This tea has much more flavor if made from dried leaves. Many claim it tastes very much like Oriental tea. However, this tea is more wholesome than the Oriental tea, since it has no caffeine as do the cultivated teas.

LABRADOR TEA (*Ledum groenlandicum*) p. 109

This three-foot-high shrub bears two-inch leaves that are woolly underneath. When crushed, they give forth a pleasant aroma. Gather the leaves, and dry them. Steep as you would any tea. Angier states that for some people this tea has a cathartic effect. Medsger warns that not more than one cup should be drunk at one time.

SWEET ANISE
(*Foeniculum vulgare; Osmorhiza occidentalis*) p. 94

Sweet anise, also called sweet fennel, belongs to the parsley family. The fernlike leaves are slightly aromatic and taste slightly sweet. Italians have gathered the plant for centuries, making from it a tea of which they are particularly fond. Some Italians place a little of it in soup. Steep it in boiling water to make a delicately flavored, rather sweet tea.

BASSWOOD (*Tilia americana, cordata*) p. 109

The basswood tree is also known as linden. The flowers are white and very fragrant. Make the tea from the flowers rather than the leaves. Gather the flowers on a dry, hot day and dry them indoors. Steep as you would any tea.

OTHER TEAS

Blackberry (*Rubus nigrobaccus*), strawberry (*Fragaria virginiana, vesca*), and raspberry leaves (*Rubus odoratus, strigosus*) when tender make a delicious tea. Sweet goldenrod (*Solidago odora*) has a one-sided panicle of flowers. Gather the leaves when in bloom, dry, and steep as other tea. Catnip (*Nepeta cataria*) tea is a favorite with some. This plant is in the mint family. Gather the leaves, dry them, and steep as usual. Hemlock (*Tsuga canadensis*) and Douglas fir (*Pseudotsuga arbutifolia*) needles, especially the bright green young tips which appear in the spring, make a flavorful tea. Any coniferous tree will make good tea if you use the young needles. Horehound (*Marrubium vulgare*) leaves have been used for years by people all over the United States. Cough syrup and candy have also been made from this delightful plant. Toyon berries (*Photinia arbutifolia*) make a tea and were used by Indians as such, but I do not personally care for the flavor. I rank it the least of all the wilderness teas.

PLANTS USED FOR GARNISHES

Plants used for garnishes include the sweet bay or laurel (*Magnolia virginiana*), peppergrass (*Lepidium virginicum*), sheep sorrel (*Rumex acetosella*), watercress (*Radicula nasturtium, aquaticum; Nasturtium officinale*), wild onion (*Allium cernuum*), and wild garlic (*Allium vineale*). All of these are put in salads, soups, iced drinks, etc. One warning about using fresh watercress—be sure the water in which it grows is not polluted.

CHAPTER 10

POISONOUS PLANTS

An estimated 125,000 identified wild plants are edible, while, on the other hand, only a few poisonous plants can cause death to the unsuspecting individual. I will not try to cover all poisonous plants but will cover the most common.

I quote from pages 54 and 55 of *Emergency Rescue Survival, Air Force Manual* (1962): "Edibility Rules: Never eat large quantities of strange food without first testing it. Prepare a cooked sample, then take a mouthful, chew it, and hold it in your mouth for five minutes. If it still tastes good, go ahead and eat it. If the taste is disagreeable, don't eat it. . . . A burning, nauseating, or bitter taste is a warning of danger. *A small quantity of even poisonous food is not likely to prove fatal or even dangerous,* whereas a large quantity may be. (Does not apply to mushrooms.) . . .

"In general it is safe to try foods that you observe being eaten by birds and mammals, but there are some exceptions. Food eaten by rodents (mice, rats, rabbits, beavers, squirrels, muskrats), or by monkeys, baboons, bears, raccoons, and various other omnivorous animals . . . usually will be safe for you to try. [Observe preceding caution regarding mushrooms.] As a general rule, poisonous plants are not a serious hazard, except on the rare occasion when you may accidentally walk into a patch of them. Your chances of eating a poisonous plant are rare. Frequently, only the seeds are poisonous, but use care in selecting any plant part."

If you question the safety of a food and you are desperate, be sure to follow the edibility rule as stated above. It is best to cook all questionable food, since cooking removes most poisons. (Again, this does not apply to mushrooms.) A good example of this is the buckeye. In its raw state it is poisonous. After it has been cooked and properly processed, it is perfectly safe as a food.

CONTACT POISONS

POISON IVY (*Rhus toxicodendron*) p. 109

The leaves of this plant always grow in threes. The leaves never occur in pairs along the stem. An attractive climbing vine, usually, it may also take the form of a low-growing shrub. It grows all over the United States, except the extreme West, including California, Nevada, the tip of Oregon and Idaho, and the western tip of Utah and Arizona. The oak-leaf form of poison ivy grows in the Eastern and Southern states and is more distinctive than other types. It does not usually climb as a vine but is a low-growing shrub.

Poison ivy produces a rash upon contact or when one is exposed to its smoke as it burns. Some people are so allergic that they will be affected by only walking where it grows profusely. Others will get a rash by petting dogs or cats that have walked through poison ivy. I will not recommend a specific treatment for poison-ivy rash. Gibbons states that the juice from jewelweed (*Impatiens biflora*) which has been rubbed between the palms of the hands and applied to the skin which has contacted poison ivy will keep the rash from forming. Others say the tea from manzanita leaves is good when rubbed on the affected part. Still others say to wash immediately with strong soap and water, and the rash will not develop. Still others go to their physician to procure a cortisone ointment which seems very effective. I suppose you have heard of many more "sure cures" for poison ivy.

POISON OAK (*Rhus diversiloba*) no illus.

This plant, related to poison ivy, occurs only in the Western states, including the western half of Washington and Oregon, and more than 90 percent of California on the western side. Poison oak grows mostly as a rank, upright shrub with small, woody stems rising from the ground. It grows in abundance along roadsides and can attach itself to upright objects such as a telephone pole, or a conifer, taking the form of a vine. In wooded areas it principally takes the form of a vine. I have seen poison oak in Humboldt County, California, running thirty to forty feet up a redwood tree. In the fall it is a beautiful sight, causing tourists to stop and take pictures. The leaves are in three leaflets, with irregular margins. Some poison oak leaves resemble the oak leaf, thus the name poison oak, which is actually a misnomer.

POISON SUMAC (*Rhus vernix*) p. 109

The poison sumac grows as a coarse, woody shrub or small tree and never in the vinelike form of its relatives poison oak and poison ivy. It grows in the Eastern states, eastward from eastern Minnesota, northeastern Illinois, Indiana, central Kentucky and Tennessee, and southeastern Texas. The leaves of the poison sumac divide into seven to thirteen leaflets, arranged in pairs with a single leaflet at the end of the midrib. They are elongated, oval, with smooth edges. They are three to four inches long and one to two inches wide, with a smooth velvet texture. When they first appear in the spring, they are bright orange, changing to a dark green, and are glossy on the upper surface, pale green underneath, with scarlet midribs. They turn to a brilliant red-orange or russet shade in the fall.

Do not confuse poison sumac (*Rhus vernix*) with the nonpoisonous varieties or species such as the smooth sumac (*Rhus glabra*), staghorn sumac (*Rhus typhina*), and dwarf sumac (*Rhus copallina*). All of the nonpoisonous sumac species have red fruits that form a distinctive terminal seed head. The poisonous sumac (*Rhus vernix*) has slender hanging clusters of white fruit. Remember, the poisonous sumac leaves have fewer leaflets, are more oval-shaped, and have smooth margins.

MECHANICAL IRRITANTS

STINGING NETTLE (*Urtica dioica*) p. 94

Stinging nettle grows quite high, from three to five feet, with ovate leaves which are somewhat heart-shaped. The stems are thickly covered with stinging hairs. Although this nettle will irritate the skin so that it will burn for twenty-four to forty-eight hours, it is not classified as a poisonous plant. Care should be taken, however, when picking the tender leaves for greens. Probably you should wear gloves.

PRICKLY PEAR
(*Opuntia vulgaris; Rafinesquii basilaris*) p. 104

Prickly pears have very fine, spiny bristles which can be very annoying when picking the cactus fruit. Also avoid the sharp spines on the leaves. Although annoying and irritating, they are not considered poisonous.

COMMON POISONOUS PLANTS

A few poisonous plants need a little more description than most of the others I shall list.

WHITE CAMAS (*Zygadenus venenosus*) p. 110

This plant is a relative to the blue camas (*Camassia quamash*). The blue camas bulb is edible and a great favorite of many Indian tribes. However, the bulb of the white camas (*Zygadenus venenosus*), sometimes known as death camas, is very poisonous. Death camas has a white flower, grows from one to two feet tall, and bears dull green leaves which are folded lengthwise, having rough edges. It usually grows in meadows. The white or sometimes cream-colored flowers are small, less than one-half inch in diameter, and are striped with green on the outside.

JACK-IN-THE-PULPIT (*Arisaema triphyllum*) p. 110

This plant has a starchy bulb which stings and burns when eaten. Even after boiling, it retains its burning taste. Medsger states, however, that he boiled the bulbs, dried them for several weeks, ground them into meal, and, when they were baked into cakes as the Indians did, found them pleasant to the taste and very nutritious.

HEMLOCK
(*Cicuta douglasii, bolanderi; Conium maculatum*) p. 110

Water hemlock (*Cicuta*) and poison hemlock (*Conium*), both poisonous, are members of the carrot or parsley family, Umbelliferae. Do not confuse them with true hemlocks, which are coniferous trees of the pine family, Pinaceae. (If you want further reading, I would suggest Circular 530, Division of Agricultural Sciences, University of California at Davis.)

The rootstalks of water hemlock are poisonous, and the green leaves, stems, and fruit of the poison hemlock are poisonous, especially to livestock. The leaves of poison hemlock very largely lose their toxicity when dried. Poison hemlock is not nearly as toxic as water hemlock.

MAYAPPLE (*Podophyllum peltatum*) p. 103

The mayapple, also called mandrake, is considered by some to be quite edible and not at all poisonous. However, I have a friend who ate only two and landed deathly ill in the hospital. It can produce a very severe colic. Some suggest that the mayapple be eaten with caution. The root is especially potent. Indians used the root as a medicine, but we are cautioned to be very careful when using the root or when eating the fruit.

OLEANDER
(Nerium oleander; Thervetia peruviana, nerifolia) p. 110

Almost everyone knows that all parts of the oleander are poisonous. By that I mean leaves, stems, fruit, and root. But I am not sure that everyone realizes how deadly it can be. One group of young people in northern California went on a wiener roast. Some of them speared their wieners with oleander stems, for they grew nearby. In a very short time several were rushed to the hospital with severe stomach cramps. Three out of five died, and the other two were very seriously ill for a long time. Oleander is beautiful but deadly.

CASTOR BEANS *(Ricinus communis)* p. 110

The beautiful castor bean grows wild along roads and streams all over America. Many people plant it in their gardens to keep the gophers away. Since it is a decorative plant, some people plant it just because it is so beautiful. Little do most people realize just how dangerous the castor bean plant is. Two or three beans eaten by a child can cause his death, and as few as six can cause the death of an adult.

NIGHTSHADE *(Solanum douglasii, xanti)* p. 111

The berries of both the white nightshade *(douglasii)* and the purple nightshade *(xanti)* are poisonous. The berries of the white nightshade are black, while the purple nightshade berries are pale green or purple, about the size of a very small cherry. These berries are toxic enough to cause the death of a child or an adult. All parts are poisonous.

LARKSPUR
(Delphinium scaposum, Hanseni, bicolor, etc.) p. 111

There are many species of larkspur, and all parts are poisonous. Larkspur poisoning, from eating any part, will cause a fall in blood pressure, weak pulse, and convulsions.

HYDRANGEA
(*Hydrangea hortensis, aborescens, radiata,* etc.) p. 111

Remember that the poisoning from any part of the hydrangea will cause severe headache, respiratory stimulation, tachycardia (fast pulse), and convulsions.

POKEWEED (*Phytolacca americana*) p. 92

This plant is included among poisonous plants, although most Southerners use it for greens. It can be poisonous. The large, older leaves when picked and placed in a blender for a green drink nearly took the lives of a couple I know. Remember, choose the tender young leaves for your greens. These are perfectly harmless when cooked until tender.

MUSHROOMS

This important subject is so vast that I will not go into any detail whatsoever or point out that certain mushrooms are poisonous and certain ones are perfectly safe. I would suggest *The Mushroom Hunter's Field Guide,* by Alexander H. Smith, Ann Arbor, The University of Michigan Press, 1963, revised edition ($8.95). This is the best book I have ever run across on this subject. It has hundreds of illustrations, both black and white and colored plates, plus a very detailed description of each species.

Heed the caution given in the book *How to Survive on Land and Sea,* United States Naval Institute, Anapolis, Maryland, 1965 ($4.50), on page 59: "*Many mushrooms are edible and may furnish a source of food, particularly in temperate regions; but no species should be tried unless you are sure of its identity, for some species are deadly poisonous.* The most widespread among the dangerously poisonous mushrooms are the Amanitas which have a frill or ring (veil) around the upper part of the stem, a bag (volva) at the bottom, and a white spore deposit which drops out of the gills.

"Don't try eating any mushroom that possesses these three characteristics. Amanitas almost always grow on the ground in the woods or shade. . . . Puffballs are more or less globular bodies that develop their spores inside and have a solid white interior when young. *All are edible when fresh.* . . . Avoid eating all fungi in the button or unexpanded stage. *Morel mushrooms are easily recognized and all are edible.*"

The *Emergency Rescue Survival, Air Force Manual,* page 58, states, "*Edible mushrooms sometimes have the frill or ring, but never the cup.* . . . When picking young mushrooms, don't mistake them for young puffballs, which are edible but without gills and central stem. To be certain, cut the young 'button' vertically and look for gills and cup. *If you find a poisonous kind (always with gills), cooking will not destroy the poisonous properties.*"

PROTECT THE CHILDREN

Some of the most beautifully kept gardens in America are actually hazardous areas for small children who have not been taught by their parents to keep plants out of their mouths. Teach children early not to eat any plant parts—leaves, berries, seeds, stems, or flowers—other than those plants commonly used for food. Adults should also be cautious about making "medicinal" concoctions from plants unless they are very sure which parts are edible and under what conditions they are safe to use.

Certain parts of the plants we find in our vegetable gardens are poisonous. For example, the leaf of the rhubarb plant, the stalks of which are used to make sauce or pie filling, is one of the most poisonous leaves. It contains oxalic acid, which may cause severe damage to the kidneys. Large amounts of raw rhubarb leaves can cause convulsions, coma, and eventual death.

Unripe huckleberries and leaves, or the green skin of Irish potatoes, are mildly poisonous. The roots of the common elderberry bush can cause nausea and digestive disturbances. The elderberry fruit, on the other hand, is perfectly safe to eat, cooked or raw. The beautiful Christmas poinsettia contains an acrid, burning juice that will kill a child if he eats one leaf! Mistletoe berries have caused both children and adults to lose their lives. The delicate and fragrant lily of the valley, both leaves and flowers, can cause an irregular heartbeat and pulse, accompanied by a digestive upset and even mental confusion. The seedpod of the bird-of-paradise flower may cause nausea, vomiting, and diarrhea.

Some plants contain large amounts of tannic acid. Acorns and the fruit of the buckeye plant are examples. Children must not be allowed to chew on acorns. Both the acorn and buckeye must be properly leached or processed, rendering them perfectly safe to eat. Berries from the daphne plant are poisonous. Just a few berries can kill a child. Wisteria seeds or pods poison many children each year. The bulbs from hyacinth, amaryllis (naked lady), narcissus, and daffodil are poisonous. Many people have the mistaken idea that all bulbs are edible. They are not.

I know I have painted a somewhat depressing picture. However, may I remind you that, as mentioned in the first paragraph of this chapter, approximately 125,000 known, identified wild plants are edible and only a few in comparison are poisonous. I have purposely included some of the cultivated plants because they are common.

PLANTS WITH POISONOUS PARTS

Autumn crocus: bulb
Azalea: all parts
Baneberry: berries, white or red
Bird-of-paradise flower: seedpod
Bittersweet: berries
Black locust: bark, sprouts, foliage

Bleeding heart: leaves, tubers
Bluebonnet: seeds
Buckeye: unprocessed seed
Buttercup: all parts
Camara (red sage): green berries
Camas, white: bulb
Castor bean: seeds
Cherry: seeds, leaves
Columbine: berries
Cyclamen: tuber
Daffodil: bulbs
Daphne: bark, leaves, fruit
Delphinium: young plant, seeds
Desert marigold: whole plant
Dumb cane: all parts, especially leaves and
    tubers
Dutchman's-breeches: leaves, tubers
Elderberry: leaves, shoots, bark
Elephant's ear: all parts
English holly: berries
False hellebore: whole plant, especially leaves
Flax: white plant, especially seedpods
Four-o'clock: root, seed
Foxglove: leaves
Garden huckleberry: unripe berries, leaves
Golden chain: beanlike seed capsules
Hemlock (poison): green leaves, stems, fruit
Hemlock (water): rootstalks, dry or fresh
Hyacinth: bulb
Hydrangea: leaves
Iris: underground stems
Ivy: leaves
Jack-in-the-pulpit: all parts, especially roots
Jasmine: berries
Jimsonweed: all parts
Lantana: foliage (all parts)
Larkspur: young plants, seeds

Laurel: all parts, except leaves
Lily of the valley: leaves, flowers
Lupine: leaves
Mayapple: apple, foliage, roots
Milkweed: raw leaves, stems
Mistletoe: all parts, especially the berries
Mock orange: fruit
Monkshood: root
Moonflower: seeds
Moonseed: berries
Narcissus: bulbs
Nightshade: leaves and unripe berries
Oak: foliage, unprocessed acorns
Oleander: leaves, branches
Peach: seeds, leaves
Philodendron: stem, leaves
Pimpernel: all parts
Pinks: seed
Plum: seed, leaves
Poinsettia: leaves, stems, sap
Poison ivy and oak: leaves
Pokeweed: raw leaves when plant is old
Potato (Irish): green skin, new sprouts
Rhododendron: all parts
Rhubarb: leaves
Scotch broom: seed
Sneezeweed: whole plant
Snow-on-the-mountain: milky sap
Spanish bayonet: root
Spider lily: bulb
Star-of-Bethlehem: bulbs
Sweet pea: stem
Toadstools: whole plant
Toyon: leaves
Wild grape: root
Wisteria: seeds, pods
Yew: berries, foliage

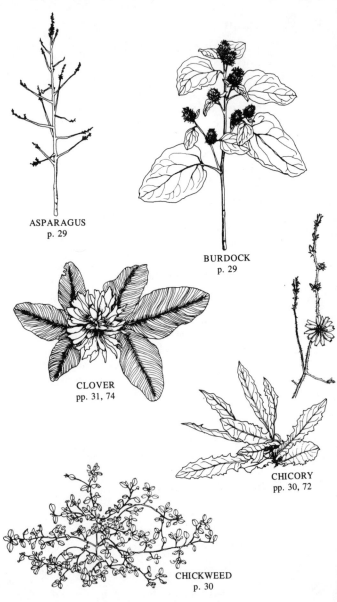

ASPARAGUS
p. 29

BURDOCK
p. 29

CLOVER
pp. 31, 74

CHICORY
pp. 30, 72

CHICKWEED
p. 30

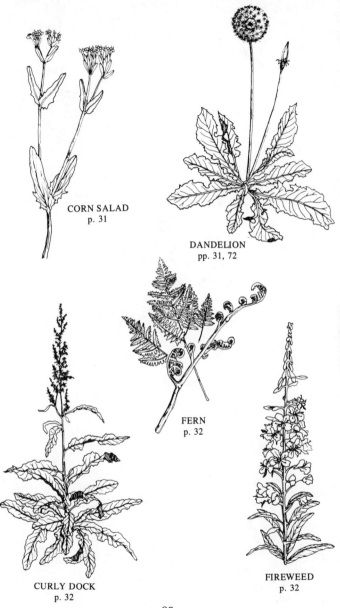

CORN SALAD
p. 31

DANDELION
pp. 31, 72

FERN
p. 32

CURLY DOCK
p. 32

FIREWEED
p. 32

89

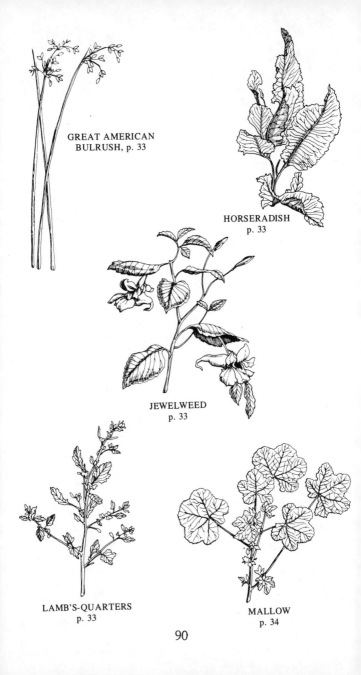

GREAT AMERICAN
BULRUSH, p. 33

HORSERADISH
p. 33

JEWELWEED
p. 33

LAMB'S-QUARTERS
p. 33

MALLOW
p. 34

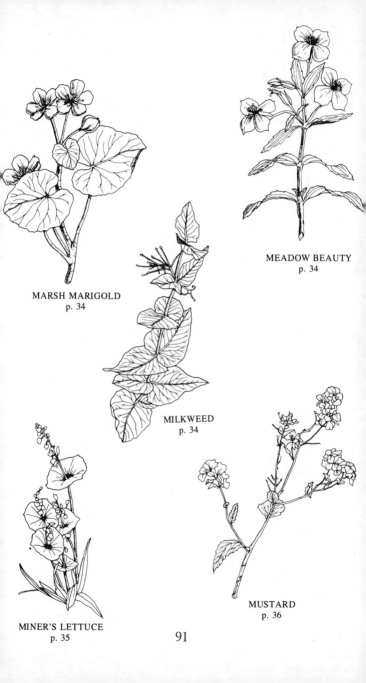

MEADOW BEAUTY
p. 34

MARSH MARIGOLD
p. 34

MILKWEED
p. 34

MUSTARD
p. 36

MINER'S LETTUCE
p. 35

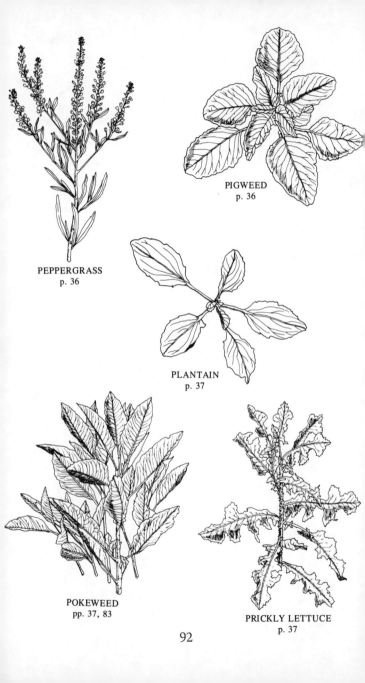

PEPPERGRASS
p. 36

PIGWEED
p. 36

PLANTAIN
p. 37

POKEWEED
pp. 37, 83

PRICKLY LETTUCE
p. 37

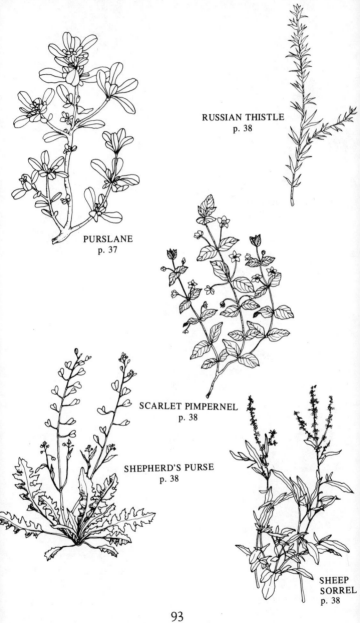

RUSSIAN THISTLE
p. 38

PURSLANE
p. 37

SCARLET PIMPERNEL
p. 38

SHEPHERD'S PURSE
p. 38

SHEEP
SORREL
p. 38

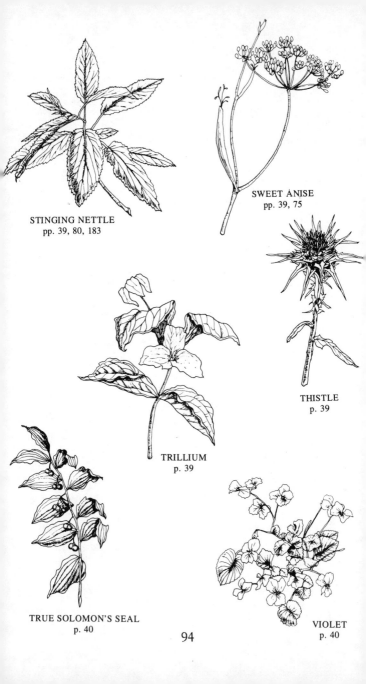

STINGING NETTLE
pp. 39, 80, 183

SWEET ANISE
pp. 39, 75

THISTLE
p. 39

TRILLIUM
p. 39

TRUE SOLOMON'S SEAL
p. 40

VIOLET
p. 40

94

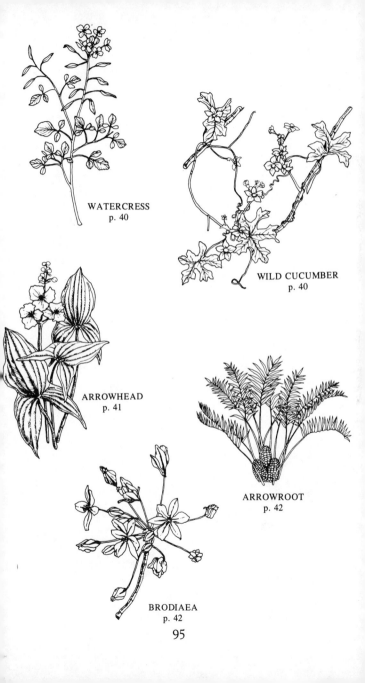

WATERCRESS
p. 40

WILD CUCUMBER
p. 40

ARROWHEAD
p. 41

ARROWROOT
p. 42

BRODIAEA
p. 42

95

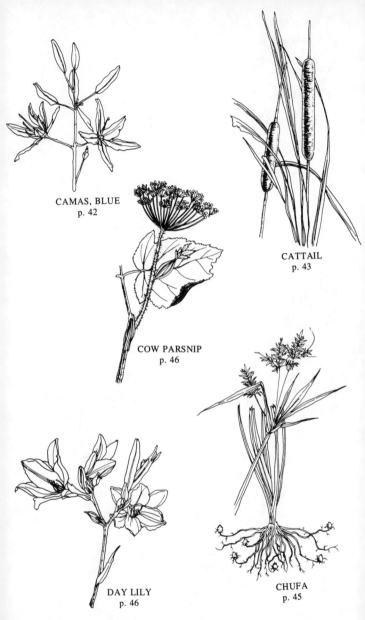

CAMAS, BLUE
p. 42

CATTAIL
p. 43

COW PARSNIP
p. 46

DAY LILY
p. 46

CHUFA
p. 45

96

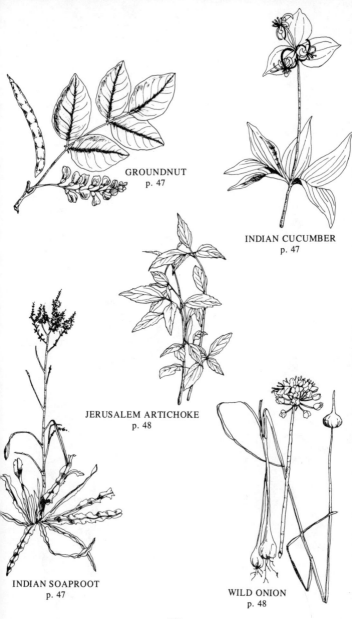

GROUNDNUT
p. 47

INDIAN CUCUMBER
p. 47

JERUSALEM ARTICHOKE
p. 48

INDIAN SOAPROOT
p. 47

WILD ONION
p. 48

WATER LILY
p. 48

SALSIFY
p. 49

POTATO VINE
p. 48

RICE ROOT
p. 49

PRAIRIE TURNIP
p. 49

98

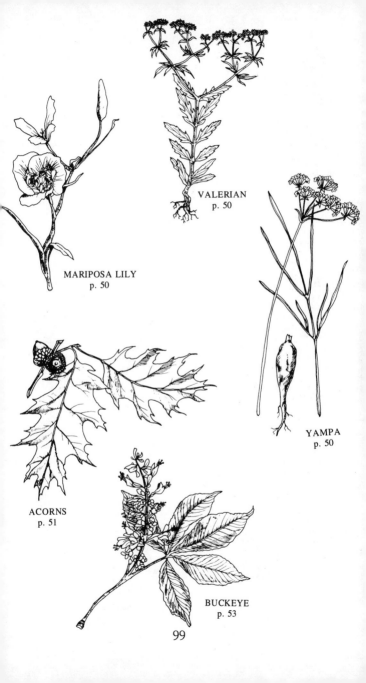

VALERIAN
p. 50

MARIPOSA LILY
p. 50

YAMPA
p. 50

ACORNS
p. 51

BUCKEYE
p. 53

99

BEECHNUT
p. 54

HAZELNUT
p. 56

BLACK WALNUT
p. 55

BUTTERNUT
p. 55

CHESTNUT
p. 55

HICKORY
p. 56

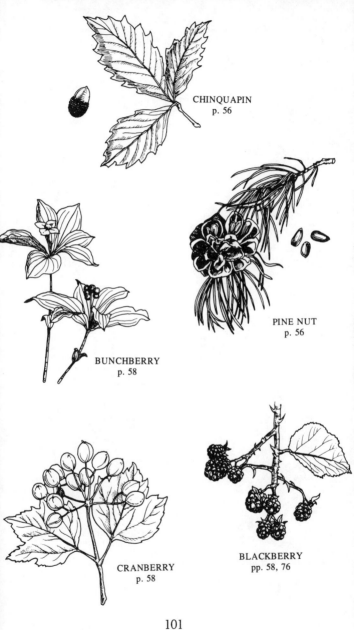

CHINQUAPIN
p. 56

PINE NUT
p. 56

BUNCHBERRY
p. 58

CRANBERRY
p. 58

BLACKBERRY
pp. 58, 76

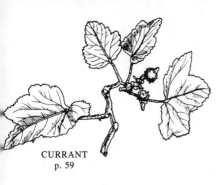

CURRANT
p. 59

ELDERBERRY
p. 59

CHOKECHERRY
p. 58

GOOSEBERRY
p. 60

DEWBERRY
p. 59

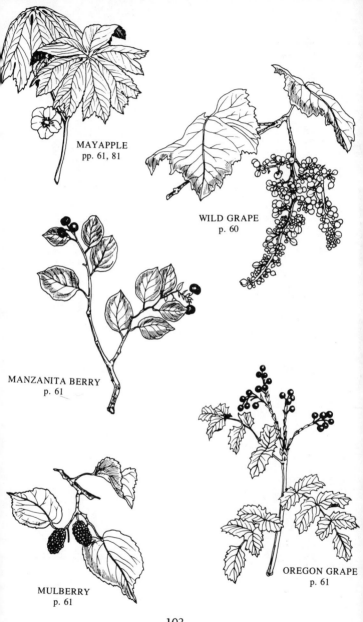

MAYAPPLE
pp. 61, 81

WILD GRAPE
p. 60

MANZANITA BERRY
p. 61

OREGON GRAPE
p. 61

MULBERRY
p. 61

103

PASSIONFLOWER
p. 62

PYRACANTHA
p. 63

RASPBERRY
pp. 63, 76

PRICKLY PEAR
pp. 62, 80

SERVICEBERRY
p. 64

SALMONBERRY
p. 64

STRAWBERRY
pp. 64, 76

TOYON BERRY
pp. 65, 76

THIMBLEBERRY
p. 64

IRISH MOSS
p. 67

TWINBERRY
p. 65

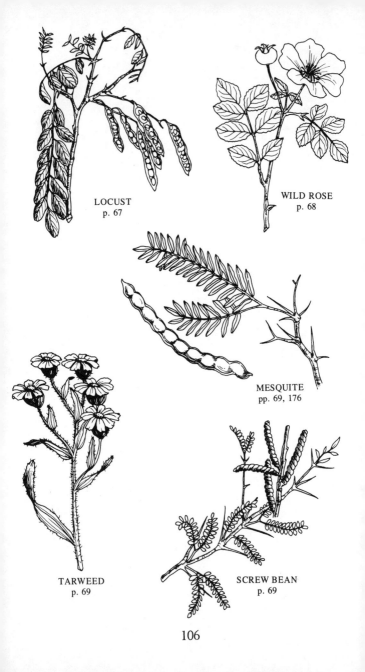

LOCUST
p. 67

WILD ROSE
p. 68

MESQUITE
pp. 69, 176

TARWEED
p. 69

SCREW BEAN
p. 69

106

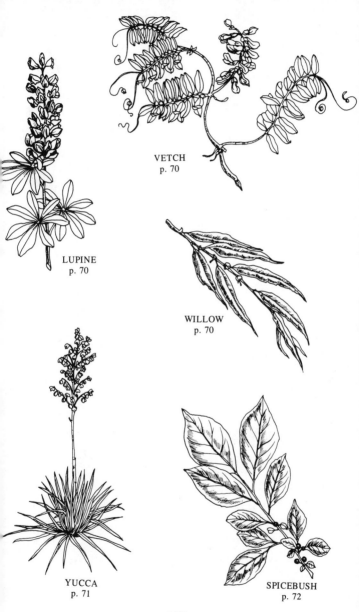

VETCH
p. 70

LUPINE
p. 70

WILLOW
p. 70

YUCCA
p. 71

SPICEBUSH
p. 72

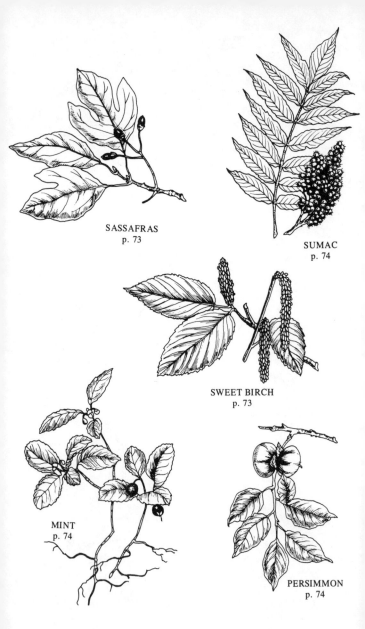

SASSAFRAS
p. 73

SUMAC
p. 74

SWEET BIRCH
p. 73

MINT
p. 74

PERSIMMON
p. 74

NEW JERSEY TEA
p. 75

POISON IVY
(poisonous) p. 78

BASSWOOD
p. 76

POISON SUMAC
(poisonous) p. 79

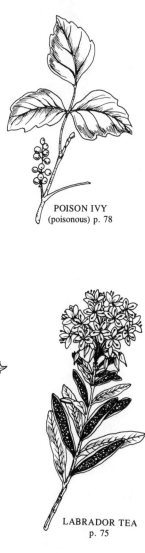

LABRADOR TEA
p. 75

WHITE (DEATH) CAMAS
(poisonous) pp. 42, 80

HEMLOCK
(poisonous) p. 81

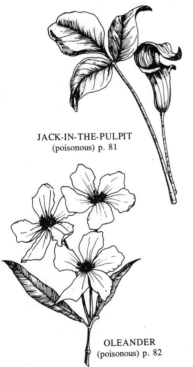

JACK-IN-THE-PULPIT
(poisonous) p. 81

CASTOR B
(poisonous)

OLEANDER
(poisonous) p. 82

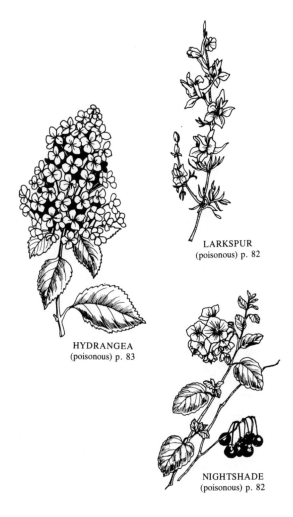

LARKSPUR
(poisonous) p. 82

HYDRANGEA
(poisonous) p. 83

NIGHTSHADE
(poisonous) p. 82

CHAPTER 11

WILDERNESS COOKERY

Just because you find yourself in the wilderness does not mean that you have to eat your food raw. Even if you have no utensils, there are ways to cook food, and cooking renders food more digestible and more palatable. How would you like to eat dry beans, wheat, or rice? Cooking also destroys bacteria and toxins and such unpleasantness as bitterness caused by tannin in acorns and buckeye. Although boiling destroys many poisons, remember that this does not apply to mushrooms.

Elevation affects the boiling of water. The higher the altitude, the longer it takes to boil food. Do not try to boil water at 12,000 feet or higher.

If you have plenty of food, an abundance of water, and a good fire, you still must have something in which to cook your food. There are several ways you can cook without the utensils which we are accustomed to using. Food can be boiled, roasted, steamed, or dried.

BOILING WITHOUT UTENSILS

SCOOPED-OUT LOG

If you have something you wish to boil, or if you need merely to boil some water and find yourself with everything you need but a kettle, all is not lost. Find a small log about eight to ten inches in diameter. Scoop it out, making a vessel which will hold nearly a quart of water. Light a fire, heating some small, clean stones. Secure a green pliable twig, and make prongs with which to transfer the hot stones from the fire to the vessel you have just made. Adding the hot stones to the water which you have placed in your scooped-out log will produce boiling water in a very few minutes. Now you may go ahead and boil the vegetable or whatever you had in mind to cook. The log should be green, if possible, so that it will not burn through should you decide to place it on coals, which can be done if the bottom is not too thick. (It can't be too thin, either!) Indians have used this scooped-out-log method for centuries.

CLAY PIT

If you can find some good-quality clay, you can make a clay pit, heat some stones, fill the pit with the amount of water you need, add the hot stones, and you are in business! This will work only with clay or adobe.

BAMBOO SECTIONS

If in the tropics or where large bamboo grows, you will be happy to know that you can use this versatile plant for cooking purposes. Of course, gourds and half of a coconut shell will serve equally as well. Coming back to the bamboo, I was amazed in 1968 to find a large grove of bamboo growing in Calistoga, California. I asked for a stalk four inches across, telling the lady what I wanted it for, and I now have myself some "kettles" made of bamboo.

When you have cut down a large stalk, cut the sections as follows: Cut one end just below a joint and the other just below the next upper joint. This gives you a container solid at the bottom and open at the top. I received a letter from Matias Gazan, a Filipino R.N. now living in Canada, telling me how his people in the Philippines cook with bamboo. They cut it as I described, except that they make the upper cut above the joint, thus making a completely sealed container. Then they cut a small opening in the top in which to place their food. First they put green leaves in the bottom of the vessel, place their food next, packing it well, then put green leaves on top, sealing it by tying it securely. Then they place the sealed container in the bed of coals and let it cook, turning it every so often so that it won't burn through on one side. It takes approximately twenty minutes to cook most food this way. This is a good utensil to use if you want to boil your water to destroy bacteria.

BIRCH BARK

Cooking vessels can be made out of bark. The bark most commonly used by both woodsmen and Indians of old is birch bark. "Cut a twelve-inch square of bark. Make two diagonal folds between all four corners, open them up, turn the bark over, and fold it in thirds. Open again and fold in thirds the other way. Then pinch up each corner so that the triangle is pointing out. Fold this along the side, and pin in place with a thorn, or sliver of wood. Make sure your bark contains no holes."— *How to Survive on Land and Sea,* p. 114. When your bark vessel is finished, put water in it and place over a bed of coals or a small fire. The vessel will not catch on fire below the water level, so keep the fire small or use hot coals. Or you can add hot stones to the water until it boils, and cook that way.

INDIAN HOLLOW STONE

Nearly everyone has seen and many own an Indian grinding stone, which is like a mortar and pestle. Mrs. Myrtle McCoy, an Indian woman living in Ukiah, California, attended one of my edible plant lectures in that city. She later sent me a tape recording, telling me many Indian secrets on food and its preparation. She told me how her mother and grandmother used to go out in the field gathering edible plants. She also told me how the Indians made their grinding stones. They chose a good solid-looking rock for the vessel. Then they took a flint or other very hard rock and ground it hollow to a depth which was suitable for cooking or for grinding their maize, etc. Some of these stones are so large that they cannot be easily transported. Drs. Grace and Henry Devnich, of Livermore, California, have such a large stone. Others range from the very small to one which will hold about two quarts of water. Hot stones were placed in this stone vessel and the water brought to a boil, and the food cooked just as well as in your own kitchen.

ANIMAL HIDE

If you have found a freshly killed animal, use its well-cleaned hide to line a hole in the ground. Water can be added, along with hot stones from your fire, and you are ready to cook your food.

STEAMING IN A HOLE

Scoop out a hole in the ground, and line with stones. Do not use stones from a stream bed, for they may contain water which, turning to steam, may cause an explosion. Build a fire over the stones lining the bottom, and let it burn down to hot coals. Cover the coals with green leaves, damp grass, or seaweed. Put in your food to be cooked, and cover again with green leaves and a layer of sand or loam or whatever kind of soil is available. Punch a hole through the earth and leaves to the food so that you can add water. Seal again after adding the water so that the food can steam. This method requires several hours before the food will be done. Indians sometimes let their food steam all night or while they were away on a hunt.

BAKING IN COALS

Wrap your food in leaves or clay. Cover the wrapped food with hot coals, cover the coals with earth, and let it bake. You will learn from experience how long it will take to cook your food. My first attempts were sorry disappointments, for I was always too anxious to uncover my food, and nearly always it was only half done.

You will soon learn when to take it out so that the food will be tender. If you dig a pit and line it with stones, following the above directions, you will find that your food will cook much quicker because the pit holds the heat better.

BAKING IN ASHES

The natives in almost every country in the world have used this method for centuries. Build a fire with softwood or any wood which will leave lots of ashes. Wrap your food in leaves, and bury it in the ashes. Potatoes or other wild tubers will bake without wrapping. When we were young, my brother and I baked potatoes this way many a time. I admit most of them were half done, for we did not have the patience to wait long enough to allow them to become tender. If done right, you will have results which your own modern oven cannot equal.

BAKING ON A STICK

Choose a green hardwood stick, pierce the food through, and hold it over the coals of your fire. Keep the food as close to the coals as you can without burning it or catching it on fire. Bake campfire bread by this method.

DRYING

Dry food by sun or fire or by just letting it dry in the air. A good wind will dry the food fairly fast. Fruit and tubers dry with great success if you slice them into thin sections. The Indians dried acorns, maize, and grass seeds, ground them into meal, and made pinole.

CHAPTER 12

RECIPES USING WILD FOODS

If isolated over a long period of time, our lot will be much more pleasant if we have a knowledge of edible plants, how to prepare or process them, and what parts to eat. I have included some recipes which you can combine with familiar ingredients from your kitchen. These are not the recipes you would use if stranded in the wilderness. I am trying only to entice you to go out into the field, get acquainted with certain edible wild plants, and experiment *now* so that when the time comes when you must rely upon these very plants, you will know how to prepare them. In preceding chapters I have gone into detail with every plant described as to how to prepare and cook it, so I will not repeat. If you are interested in a certain plant and how to prepare it, look it up in the index.

VEGETABLE RECIPES

WILD ASPARAGUS CUSTARD

1½ pounds wild asparagus
3 slices bread
1 cup Cheddar cheese, shredded
2 eggs, slightly beaten
2 cups milk, scalded
1 teaspoon salt
1 tablespoon melted margarine

Clean wild asparagus well, and cut off 2-inch tips to be used later. Cut the crisp part of the remaining stalks

117

into 1-inch pieces. Toast the bread, and cut in 1-inch squares. Arrange alternate layers of bread squares, asparagus, and cheese in a shallow casserole. Combine the eggs, milk, salt, and melted margarine. Pour over the casserole contents, and bake 45 minutes in a 325-degree oven, or until the custard sets. At the same time salt the reserved tips, and wrap them in a square of aluminum foil. Fold the edges to seal, and put them in the oven with the casserole. Unwrap and arrange on top of the custard before serving.

THISTLE CASSEROLE

        4 cups thistle stems, sliced in diagonals
           Boiling water
        3 tablespoons margarine
        3 tablespoons flour
     1½ cups vegetarian chicken broth
        ½ cup cream or undiluted evaporated milk
           Salt to taste
        ½ cup wild nuts, chopped fine
        2 tablespoons cheese, grated
        2 tablespoons fine bread crumbs

With gloves on, cut tender, juicy stalks of thistle. Peel the outer layer of the stems, saving the tender inner core. Cut in diagonal slices. Place in a kettle, and cover with boiling water. Let it come to a boil again. Drain immediately. Make a cream sauce by melting the margarine, blending in the flour, and gradually adding the vegetable chicken broth and cream (or milk). Season the cream sauce to taste, stir in the chopped wild nuts (hazelnuts are excellent). Pour over the cooked thistle, which has been placed in a casserole. Combine the grated cheese and bread crumbs to make a topping. Bake 20 minutes in a 375-degree oven, or until brown and bubbling.

BUCKEYE CASSEROLE

- 2 cups processed buckeye meal (may use 1 medium eggplant, cubed and cooked)
- ¼ cup salad oil
- 1 onion, chopped fine
- 1 medium green pepper, cut in ¼-inch cubes
- 1 tomato, skinned and chopped
- ½ teaspoon each of basil and oregano
- ½ teaspoon salt
- ½ cup bread crumbs
- 2 tablespoons margarine

Heat the oil in a skillet, and sauté the onion. Stir in the processed buckeye meal, green pepper, tomato, basil, oregano, and salt. Place in an oiled casserole, cover with crumbs, and dot with margarine. Bake for 30 minutes in a 350-degree oven, or until well browned.

BUCKEYE SOUP

- 2 cups processed buckeye meal, fresh or canned
- 2 cups milk
- ¼ cup celery, chopped fine
- ¼ small bell pepper, chopped fine
- ½ medium-sized onion, chopped fine
  Salt to taste
  McKay's Chicken Style Seasoning (vegetarian) to taste
- 1 teaspoon margarine

Sauté celery, bell pepper, and onion until well done. Place buckeye meal and milk in a saucepan, and bring to a boil. Add celery, onion, and bell pepper when tender. Add salt, other seasoning, and margarine. Serve piping hot with crackers.

CATTAIL CASSEROLE

- 1 cup scraped cattail spikes, cooked
- ½ cup bread crumbs
- 1 egg, slightly beaten

½ cup milk
¼ teaspoon salt
1 teaspoon G. Washington's Seasoning and
Broth, or other seasoning.

Mix all ingredients in small, oiled casserole, and bake in a moderate oven (350 degrees) for 30 minutes, or until knife comes out clean. Serve with or without gravy.

CATTAIL SPIKES

Pick about a pound of cattail spikes. They should be picked while green and hard, just before the husk comes off. Do not pick when they begin to turn yellow. Remember, the spikes are not what you know as cattails but that portion just above the cattail. Cook in salted water the same day they are gathered. They do not hold over even one day, unless you freeze them. Butter them while hot, and eat them like corn on the cob. If you like, you may scrape off the green part from the core after cooking, and serve like any vegetable with melted margarine.

DAY LILY FLOWER BUDS

Gather as many unopened flower buds as you can use. Boil for a few minutes, and season like any vegetable. They also may be dipped in a rich egg batter and fried, or added to soups or stews.

DAY LILY TUBERS

Gather 2 cups of crisp tubers. Scrub thoroughly, and boil in salted water until tender. Slip off the skins, and serve with margarine. The raw tubers may be peeled and chopped to be used in salads.

INDIAN SOAPROOT

If tender and white, slice and cook. If old and fibrous, scrape off the soft white part from the fibers, cover with water, and cook until tender. Pour off the first water, as it will be "soapy," and boil again. Drain, and serve with melted margarine. It is also delicious creamed.

WILD SALSIFY SOUP

The roots must be tender. Scrape the roots, cut in cubes, and boil with chopped onions until tender. Add salt, milk, and margarine. Bring again to a boil, and serve with crackers.

WILD GREENS SOUFFLÉ

1½ cups any wild potherb, boiled until tender and then chopped
2 tablespoons margarine
2 tablespoons flour
½ cup milk
1 teaspoon onion juice
½ teaspoon salt
3 eggs, separated
¼ cup margarine
¼ cup flour
2 cups milk
1 teaspoon salt
¼ pound cheese, grated

Make a thick white sauce, using 2 tablespoons margarine, 2 tablespoons flour, ½ cup milk, 1 teaspoon onion juice, and ½ teaspoon salt. Cool slightly. Beat egg yolks slightly; add white sauce slowly, and stir until well blended. Add cooked wild greens, and fold in stiffly beaten egg whites. Turn into a well-buttered 4-cup ring mold which has been lined in the bottom with wax paper; set in a shallow pan of hot water, and bake in a 375-degree oven for about 30 minutes, or until a knife comes out clean. (May be baked in a greased casserole.) Meanwhile, make a white sauce with the remaining ¼ cup margarine, ¼ cup flour, and 2 cups milk. Add salt and grated cheese at the end, and stir until melted. Unmold the ring on a hot serving plate, and serve with the cheese sauce. The center of the ring may be filled with buttered or creamed wild onions.

PURSLANE CASSEROLE

   1½ cups cooked, salted purslane tips (may use processed milkweed pods, cut in 1-inch lengths)
   2 eggs, slightly beaten
   1 cup bread crumbs, toasted
   1 cup milk
   ½ teaspoon salt
   1 envelope of G. Washington's Seasoning and Broth

Mix ingredients, place in an oiled casserole, and bake in a moderate oven (350 degrees) until set. Serve at once.

ARROWHEAD SALAD

   1½ cups boiled arrowhead tubers, peeled
   Pimento
   Dill pickle
   ⅛ teaspoon celery salt
   Small amount onion, chopped fine (preferably green onions)
   Small amount olives, chopped
   Mayonnaise
   Salt to taste

Mix, chill for at least one hour, and serve.

FRUIT DISHES

ELDERBERRY PIE

   Pastry for a 2-crust pie
   3½ cups elderberries, washed and stemmed
   1 tablespoon lemon juice
   1 cup sugar
   ¼ teaspoon salt
   ⅓ cup flour
   1 tablespoon margarine

Spread elderberries in pastry-lined 9-inch pie pan. Sprinkle with lemon juice. Combine sugar, salt, and flour; sprinkle over the berries. Dot with margarine. Adjust the top crust, crimp edges, and cut vents for steam to escape. Bake in a hot oven (400 degrees) for from 35 to 40 minutes, or until juices show in vents and crust is a golden brown.

MULBERRY PIE

Pastry for a 2-crust pie
3 cups mulberries (may use 2 cups mulberries and 1 cup rhubarb, sliced thin)
1 cup sugar
4 tablespoons flour
2 tablespoons margarine

Combine sugar and flour. Sprinkle about one third of the mixture in bottom of pastry-lined 9-inch pie pan. Turn mulberries into pie pan, and add remaining sugar-flour mixture. Dot with margarine. Adjust top crust, cut steam vents, and crimp edges. Bake in a hot oven (425 degrees) for from 40 to 50 minutes, or until crust is brown and juices bubble in vents.

WILD STRAWBERRY PIE

Baked 9-inch pie shell
1½ quarts wild strawberries
1 cup sugar
3 tablespoons cornstarch
½ cup water
1 tablespoon margarine
1 cup heavy cream (or topping)
2 tablespoons sifted confectioners' sugar

Hull, wash in cold water, and thoroughly drain the wild strawberries. Crush enough (with a potato masher) to make one cup. Combine sugar and cornstarch. Add crushed berries and water. Cook over medium heat, stirring constantly, until the mixture comes to a boil.

Continue cooking and stirring over low heat for 2 minutes. The mixture will be thickened and translucent. Remove from the heat and stir in the margarine. Cool. Place whole berries in the pie shell, reserving a few choice ones for garnishing. Pour cooked mixture over berries, and chill at least 2 hours. Serve with whipped cream with confectioners' sugar added, or with topping of your choice. Garnish with remaining strawberries.

WILD FRUIT JELLY

Any wild fruit can be used in this recipe. Currants, pyracantha berries, crab apples, bunchberries, cranberries, chokecherries, gooseberries, wild grapes, and manzanita berries are examples.

Place seven cups of fruit in a 4-quart saucepan. Add 1 cup water, heat slowly to boiling, then cook briskly for about 5 minutes. Turn into a jelly bag, and let the juice drip until there are 2½ cups of juice. Do not squeeze the bag, or your jelly will not be clear. (Save pulp and the rest of the juice, if any, for jam.) Heat juice to boiling in washed saucepan, add 2 cups sugar, and boil rapidly for from 3 to 5 minutes, or until the juice gives the jelly test—two drops flow in sheet from metal spoon. Quickly skim, and pour into hot, sterilized jelly glasses. Cover immediately with a thin film of melted paraffin. When cold, add another layer of paraffin. This will make four or five small glasses of jelly.

WILD FRUIT JAM

Approximately 2 cups fruit pulp
1½ to 2 cups sugar, depending on how sour pulp is
3 tablespoons lemon juice, if needed

Rub through a sieve the pulp left from making jelly. Add an equal amount of sugar, or a little less if desired. Cook with frequent stirring to a thick, jamlike consistency, about 10 minutes. Pour into hot, sterilized glasses. Seal with melted paraffin. This will make about three small glasses of jam.

BREADS

UNLEAVENED INDIAN BREAD

2¼ cups flour (the Indians used flour made from anything they could get)
1 teaspoon salt
1 cup water
    Vegetable oil (they usually used oil made from the tarweed seed)

This unusual unleavened bread is fried rather than baked. Place flour and salt in bowl. Stir in water to make a stiff dough. Turn out on a well-floured board. Knead as you would knead bread dough for about 5 minutes or until the dough is smooth and satiny. Pinch off small pieces of dough. Let them set for about 20 minutes. Roll each piece of dough paper-thin to about a 5-inch circle. Pour oil into a heavy skillet to a depth of 1 inch. Heat to 390 degrees. Fry the circles of dough, one or two at a time, until golden brown on one side. Turn, and brown other side. The dough will blister and bubble in the oil. Drain well on paper towels. Serve warm. This will make about two dozen.

ACORN MEAL BREAD

1⅔ cups milk (may use water)
3 tablespoons sugar
1 tablespoon salt
¼ cup shortening
¾ cup warm water
2 packages active yeast, or 2 cakes compressed yeast
4 cups flour
3 cups processed acorn flour

Combine milk or water, sugar, salt, and shortening in saucepan. Heat until bubbles appear around the edge and shortening melts. Cool to lukewarm. Measure warm water (¾ cup) into large mixing bowl. Sprinkle or crumble in the yeast. Stir to dissolve. Add the lukewarm milk mixture. Combine flour and acorn flour, then add to your mixture. Beat until smooth, then add enough of the remaining flour to make dough easy to handle. Turn out onto floured board. Knead for about 5 minutes, or until dough is smooth and elastic. Put dough in a large greased bowl. Turn over to bring greased side up. Cover with a damp towel. Let rise in a warm place (85 degrees), free from draft, about 1 to 1½ hours, or until doubled in bulk. Punch dough down. Let rise about 30 minutes, or until almost doubled. Grease 2 loaf pans. Punch dough down. Turn out onto board, and knead to distribute air bubbles. Divide in half. Shape each half into a loaf, and place in the loaf pans. Cover. Let rise for about an hour, or until doubled in bulk. Bake at 425 degrees about 25 to 30 minutes, or until done.

PROTEIN DISHES

I would like to give you some of my favorite recipes, which I have modified by using wild nuts in place of walnuts, almonds, pecans, or cashews. You may experiment, using your own favorite recipes, as I did.

WILD NUT CASSEROLE

    2 tablespoons oil
    1 cup Vegetable Skallops or other gluten product
    2 tablespoons food yeast
    ½ cup onion, chopped
  1½ cups celery, chopped
    1 cup wild nuts
    1 cup crisp chow mein noodles
    2 tablespoons water
    1 can mushroom soup

Fry Skallops or gluten after dipping in breading meal or food yeast. Sauté onions and celery. Place in mixing bowl, adding chopped wild nuts and noodles. Mix well.

Place in oiled casserole. Mix 2 tablespoons water with the can of mushroom soup, and mix until smooth. Pour over ingredients in casserole. Bake for 20 minutes at 350 degrees.

CHEESE CROQUETTES

1 cup cottage cheese
1/3 cup chopped green pepper
1 cup milk
1 cup fine bread crumbs
1 cup fine acorn meal, processed, or wild nuts
2 tablespoons onion, chopped
    A mixture of milk and eggs for a dip (separate from milk above)

Mix all ingredients together (except for the egg and milk mixture), form into croquettes, and dip in the mixture of milk and eggs, then into bread crumbs. Place in oiled pan, and bake in hot oven until done.

VEGETARIAN HAMBURGERS

2 cups bread crumbs
2 potatoes, raw
2/3 cup processed fine acorn meal, or chopped wild nuts
1 teaspoon salt
1 teaspoon Vegex or other similar preparation
1 onion, chopped and sautéed in margarine
2 eggs

Soak bread crumbs which have been cut in 1-inch squares. Grind potatoes. Mix all ingredients together, form into patties, and either cook in deep fat or bake in the oven.

WILD NUT LOAF

2 cups cooked rice
2 tablespoons chopped onion
1 tablespoon Vegex or other similar preparation
1 cup tomato puree

    1 cup cream, or ½ cup evaporated milk and ½
      cup water
¼ cup wild nuts or acorn meal
2 eggs

Sauté onions in margarine; add Vegex, tomato puree, and cream or evaporated milk. Add rice and acorn meal (or nuts). Beat the two eggs well, and add to the mixture. Salt to taste, being careful not to get too salty. After mixing ingredients well, place in oiled casserole, and bake until well done. Slice, and serve with mushroom sauce or gravy.

Acorn Loaf

2 cups celery, chopped
1 tablespoon onion
3 cups milk
4 eggs
¼ cup parsley, chopped
1 cup acorn meal (may use nuts)
¼ cup melted margarine
  Salt
2 cups bread crumbs (whole-wheat bread pre-
   ferred)

Sauté celery and onions in margarine (not the ¼ cup). Mix all ingredients, and place in loaf pan. Bake until knife comes out clean.

Acorn Meat Balls

½ cup acorn meal (may use nuts)
½ cup cheese, grated
1 cup bread or cracker crumbs
1 onion, chopped fine
1 teaspoon poultry seasoning
½ teaspoon sage
3 eggs
1 can tomato sauce combined with one can
  water

Mix together, form into small balls, and fry. May use with spaghetti, or in any way you choose.

Rice and Wild Nut Patties

2 cups boiled rice
2 tablespoons margarine
2 tablespoons onion, chopped
1 cup wild nuts, chopped fine
¼ to ½ teaspoon sage
2 eggs
½ cup strained tomatoes, or ½ cup cream

Brown onion in margarine. Add all ingredients except eggs and tomatoes or cream. Mix well, then add well-beaten eggs and tomatoes or cream. Salt to taste. If too soft to roll, add fine toasted bread crumbs or cracker crumbs. Shape into patties, and brush on top with margarine or cream. Bake on oiled tin until brown. Serve with gravy or tomato sauce.

Drumsticks

½ cup mashed potatoes
1 cup boiled rice
¾ cup onion, chopped
1 teaspoon margarine
½ teaspoon sage
1 hard-boiled egg, chopped fine
½ cup wild nuts, chopped
    Salt to taste
⅔ cup bread crumbs
1 egg, beaten

Brown the onions in the margarine. Add the sage. Mix ingredients together, and shape into drumsticks, using macaroni as the bone. Roll in fine bread crumbs and egg, and fry in deep fat or in a skillet.

Lentil Loaf

2 cups cooked lentils
1 small onion, chopped

    3 tablespoons oil (or less)
    ½ cup wheat germ
    ½ cup bread crumbs
    ½ cup wild nuts, chopped
    ¾ teaspoon salt
    1 cup evaporated milk (½ cup milk, ½ cup
        water)
    1 egg

Cook lentils, and mash slightly. Sauté the onions in oil. Mix all ingredients, and bake in a 350-degree oven until done (40 to 60 minutes).

PINE NUT CASSEROLE

    2 cups vegetarian chicken slices
    1 pound thin spaghetti, cooked
    1 can mushroom soup
      Gravy from canned vege-chicken
    ¾ cup light cream
    ½ cup Cheddar cheese, grated
    ½ cup pine nuts
    1 small jar pimento, sliced thin
      Paprika

Heat together the soup, vege-chicken gravy, cream, and cheese. Mix in spaghetti, pine nuts, and pimento. Stir in the sliced vege-chicken lightly. Spread in a medium-sized casserole, sprinkle with paprika, and bake 20 minutes in a slow oven (325 degrees). Serve with buttered green peas and a tossed salad.

WILD NUT STUFFING

    1 cup chopped celery
    ¼ cup chopped onion
    4 tablespoons margarine
    2 7-ounce packages stuffing croutons, or equal
        amount fresh bread crumbs
    1 cup wild nuts, chopped

1 3-ounce can broiled, sliced mushrooms, drained
(½ cup)
3 cups hot milk

Cook celery and onion in the margarine until tender. Combine croutons, nuts, mushrooms, cooked onions, and celery. Add milk, tossing lightly. In a casserole place slices of Nuteena, Proteena, or similar vegemeat, or may use gluten steaks. Add layer of stuffing. Keep alternating until casserole is full. Bake for about 20 minutes. Some use an egg in the stuffing.

OLIVE AND RICE LOAF

2 cups wild nuts
6 slices dried bread
1 onion, medium size
1 or 2 cans ripe olives, pitted

Put these four ingredients through the food grinder. Then add:

1 cup cooked rice
1 can tomato sauce
Dash of sage
2 eggs, well beaten

Mix and bake about 1 hour. If too thick when mixed ready to bake, add some of the olive juice.

WILD NUT PIMENTO CHEESE

Soak four heaping tablespoons agar-agar in 1 cup water for 5 minutes. Cook until clear, and put in liquefier. Add one small can pimentos, drained. Liquefy ¾ cup wild nuts, 1¼ teaspoons salt, 3 tablespoons brewers' yeast, ¼ teaspoon garlic powder. Add 1 cup oil and ¼ cup lemon juice slowly. Put in square mold, and chill.

CHAPTER 13

FIRE BUILDING

CHOOSING A FIRE SITE

Perhaps the first thing of importance in making a fire is the choice of a proper site. Build your fire out in the open, if possible, with a clearing thirty feet in diameter. Rake away pine needles, leaves, or dry grass for at least ten feet around your fire. Nothing is so terrifying as a forest fire!

Never build a fire against a tree. It may be dead and catch fire, or you may injure a live tree. Try to protect your fire against wind or draft. If possible, build it against a rock or make a wall of logs. This not only protects the fire from a draft, but also serves as a reflector to direct the heat toward you or your shelter.

MAKE A SMALL FIRE

Do not build a large fire. Keep it as small as possible to serve your purpose. The smaller the fire, the less fuel it will need. Some veteran fire makers lay a foundation of sand, gravel, or flat stones upon which to build their fire. If you do use stones, be careful not to use rocks from streams, because they may crack or explode. Shale or limestone tends to do this, also. A small fire is easy to control and will not burn your food or cook it too rapidly. It also is less of a fire hazard.

WHAT MAKES A GOOD FIRE

Careful planning ensures a good fire. When you have selected your fire site, gather your tinder, kindling, and fuel. Then you must have a way to start your fire.

Having things in readiness will save you steps and perhaps failure in starting your fire. Like anything else, a good fire takes planning.

WHERE TO FIND WOOD

You will find quantities of small dead twigs under low green branches and on the trunks of small trees. Rotten trees, twigs, and hard knots (which usually are full of pitch) are plentiful. Old stumps are hard and full of pitch. Be cautious, however, not to use too much pitch in cooking, or it will flare up more than you desire. Tops of trees that lightning has struck are good to use, and they are usually fairly plentiful.

GENERAL POINTS ON FIREWOOD

Use softwoods for quick-burning fires. To distinguish between soft and hard woods, pick up one of each of those you recognize. You will notice that the hardwood weighs more because it is more compact. Use hardwoods for cooking and warmth because they burn longer and give out a steady heat. Since hardwood kindles slowly, it requires a good hot fire from softwood to get it started burning. Hardwood burns down to a good bed of coals, which is desirable for cooking. Softwood leaves a lot of ashes as a rule.

Green wood burns better in fall and winter than in the spring for some reason. Yellow birch, white ash, beech, and hickory burn better when green. Black ash, balsam, basswood (linden), box elder, and buckeye make good firedogs, backlogs, and fire banks.

TINDER

Tinder is a highly combustible substance in which a spark can be directed and fanned into a flame. Good tinder may include fine dry materials such as dry leaves, dry grasses, fuzzy or woody material you can scrape from dry plants, bird nests, bird feathers or down, finely shredded bark, wood dust produced from boring insects, dry moss, lichens, dry evergreen needles, fuzz from cat-tails, string, or any other material which will catch fire quickly and easily.

KINDLING

Kindling is a little heavier substance than tinder. Softwoods make the best kindling, even if they are smoky, short-lived, and likely to throw sparks. Examples of good kindling include thin, dry sticks of wood, dead branches which have fallen from trees, wood shavings, crumpled paper, evergreen cones which are bone-dry, or fuzz sticks, which I shall describe later. If you split ever-green wood, it will burn faster than round branches. Other softwoods which burn better when split are bass-wood (linden), alder, quaking aspen, buckeye, chestnut, cottonwood, soft maple, spruce, sycamore, tamarack, sumac, and hemlock.

Look for evergreen wood which is full of pitch, and split it up into kindling. Sticks that snap when broken are dry and make good kindling. If a stick crumbles or breaks up easily, do not use it, as it will only smolder and smoke. Split any stick over two inches in diameter if you want to use it for kindling. Store your wood in stacks near the fire so that it will dry out thoroughly.

FUEL

Fuel is the larger, heavier pieces of wood which will be the most important to gather, especially if you want a long, continuous fire for warmth or cooking. You have probably noticed that all woods do not burn the same. Some make a hot flame and burn quickly. These are usually softwoods. Some scarcely burn at all. These could be too green, or old and pithy. Other woods burn slowly, leaving a good bed of coals. These are usually hardwoods. Green wood will burn if you mix it with dry wood after your fire is burning well. Birch and white ash burn best when alive or green.

Hickory leads firewoods in heat production. Oak is

nearly as good. Beech ranks third, followed by birch and maple. Some favor ash and elm. Other hardwoods include locust, dogwood, yellow and lodgepole pine, apple, mulberry, pecan, holly, and hornbeam (ironwood). Softwoods include sumac, pine, hemlock, spruce, poplar, balsam, cedar, basswood (linden), chestnut, tamarack, alder, quaking aspen, buckeye, cottonwood, sycamore, and tulip (yellow poplar).

White fir pops and crackles and does not hold well. Alder may affect the taste of your food. Lodgepole pine is not too big and is easy to work. Dogwood holds well and is good for cooking or roasting.

LAYING A FIRE

Gather your tinder and stack your kindling and fuel before you attempt to build your fire. Collect enough wood to last as long as you will need your fire. Lay your foundation by crisscrossing several small sticks like a wigwam. Keep them far enough apart so that air can circulate freely between and under them. Pile some tinder loosely inside your little wigwam, leaving a hole on the side from which the wind blows to apply your match. Light the tinder, and when the flames carry upward toward the center, surround your wigwam with more split kindling. Then lay your larger pieces, leaving air spaces. By now you should have a good roaring fire.

HOW TO LIGHT A FIRE WITHOUT MATCHES

You should always carry waterproofed matches wherever you go, especially if you know you will be in a wilderness area for any length of time. Although you do not smoke, it is well to carry a cigarette lighter with you. The flint will make a spark even without lighter fluid, enough to catch very fine tinder afire.

HAND FIRE DRILL

If you have nothing at your disposal to light a fire, all is not lost. I will explain several methods by which you may make a fire. I would like to quote a firsthand account of an Indian's use of a hand fire drill.

"It [hand fire drill] consists of a lower and upper piece. The hearth, or lower piece, is a flat slab of wood which should be somewhat softer than the wood of the shaft or twirler. Willow or cedar make good hearths if seasoned and dry and not too old and brittle. One or more sockets are bored or gouged out with an obsidian knife to the depth of a quarter inch or so, and notched at one side. The notch leads into a shallow channel cut from the socket to the edge of the hearth.

"The drill, or upper piece, is an ordinary round stick of a size to fit the hearth socket, about the length of an arrow shaft, but larger at one end. Some Indians prefer buckeye for their drills, but they also use sagebrush, poison oak, or any hard wood. The making of fire with this drill rests upon the principle of concentration in one small spot, for only so can the human arm twirl fast and long enough to produce sufficient friction between hearth and drill to convert moving wood into heat. When ready to begin drilling, the Indian first strewed tinder—usually dried moss, or thistledown, or finely shredded inner bark of willow—along the notch and channel of the hearth and on the ground where the channel led off the board. He then squatted, holding the ends of the hearth steady against the ground with his toes, or he sometimes knelt on the hearth to hold it.

"Next he placed the drill upright, the larger end in one of the sockets, grasped it between the palms of his open hands as they were pressed together, and then rubbed back and forth in opposite directions. With each motion the drill was forced to rotate, first to the right, then to the left. His hands at the same time were bearing downward, pressing the revolving stick into the socket. Small particles of wood were ground off the sides of the socket, becoming fine sawdust or wood powder, which began to turn brown, to smoke a little, to turn darker and darker to charcoal, and to smoke in earnest, at the same time being forced by the accumulating mass out of the socket into the notch, along the channel, and so off the edge of the hearth. At this point he worked faster and faster as he approached his goal, keeping the stick whirling furiously until a tiny spark suddenly glowed within the charred and powdered wood. The effective spark formed, not in the bottom of the socket where it would be quenched by an excess of wood dust, but just outside, in the notch, from whence it traveled, spreading down the channel and onto the pile of tinder on the ground. Once this was alight, he added a small bunch of grass to it, and some coarser shavings; he blew gently on the young flame, and fire was made.

"Considerable strength and much skill are needed to achieve this result, however. The drill must be firmly and continuously pressed into the hearth—strength and coordination are both needed for this. On the other hand, too heavy a pressure at the outset will exhaust the operator's strength, so that when the crucial moment comes and the spark is nearly at hand, there is no reserve for the added push. Also as the hands bear down on the drill, they gradually slip downward along it, until, just before the hearth is touched by them, the palms must be quickly raised to the upper end of the stick. The drill actually stands still at this time, which means that the change of hand position must be done so deftly and rapidly that the heated contact point does not cool. If the hands are shifted as the spark is about to appear, the moment of no motion may prove disastrous.

"The whole process calls for manual tact of a kind that only experience can teach. The fire must be coaxed out of the unwilling wood—coaxed and nursed. Haste, violence of motion rather than strength, continuity, and rhythm will accomplish nothing, nor will indifference, lassitude, or a moment's letup. Patience, perseverance, and delicate control are precisely the requisite qualities."—Theodora Kroeber, *Ishi*.

FIRE SAW

To make the fireboard, split a piece of bamboo in two. On the inner side pick and splinter the stringy tissue until it becomes a loose mass. Just over this loose mass, on the outside of the bamboo, cut a narrow groove through and across the bamboo. To make the saw, take the other piece of split bamboo and sharpen the length of it on one side like a chisel. Hold the fireboard down with your knee while you push the saw back and forth with two hands, bearing down. Do this slowly at first, increasing your speed faster and faster, the dry powder falling on the picked tinder beneath. Then you will find that the powder will suddenly ignite into a spark. Turn the fireboard over, and fan with your hand until the tinder catches and blows into a flame.

FIRE-PLOW

Use a flat board for your fireboard. Cut a rounded groove from six to eight inches long and just wide enough to receive the fire stick. Take a sturdy stick of wood eight to ten inches long—your fire stick. Hold it in both hands. Place one end in the groove of your fireboard. Bearing down as heavy as you can, move the stick back and forth in the groove. A powder will collect in one end of the groove. The heat from the friction becomes intense enough to form a spark on the powder. Transfer the glowing powder to shredded tinder and fan into a flame. It will take experience to develop skill in making a fire, but it will work.

BOW AND DRILL

This method of fire making requires four things. First you must have a *bow* with a leather thong preferably (shoe lace can be used), long enough to loop around a dry stick which will serve as a drill. Make the bow like a regular bow with which you shoot arrows, but perhaps stiffer and with less give to it. The string for the bow is

best if made from rawhide, but anything strong and heavy will do.

Secondly, you will need a stick to serve as a *drill*. Try to find a straight hardwood stick, a little less than an inch in diameter and about a foot long (or a little longer).

Next you will need to make a *fireboard* anywhere from ten inches to a foot and a half long, about three or four inches wide, and about one inch thick. In this board cut a hole nearly an inch from the edge of the board. Start the hole and use the bow and drill to enlarge it to the right size to fit the drill. Then cut a notch from the hole to the edge of the board. It should be wider and deeper at the bottom of the notch so that it can receive the powder produced by drilling. Place some tinder at the bottom of the notch. The drill and fireboard are best when made from poplar, tamarack, basswood (linden), yucca, balsam, fir, red cedar, white cedar, cypress, cottonwood, elm, or willow. You have quite a variety of woods to choose from.

The last piece of equipment to complete your outfit is a *socket*, which you make from a small piece of hardwood just large enough to fit easily into your hand. Hollow out a little rounded indentation large enough to fit the top of your drill.

First of all, lay your firewood so that you will be ready to transfer your tinder to it. Place some tinder under the slot in the fireboard. Kneel on your right knee and place your left foot on the fireboard. Do just the opposite if you are left-handed. Take the bow in your right hand; loop the thong over the drill stick which has been set in the hole in the fireboard. Place the hollowed-out socket in your left hand, and fit it into place on top of the drill stick, exerting pressure. Keep your left wrist against your left shin and hug your left leg with your left arm. This will allow you to grip the socket more securely.

Now press down on the drill stick and begin whirling the drill by sawing back and forth with the bow. Make your draw as long as your thong will permit. To increase the friction, you might drop a few grains of sand into the hole in the fireboard. Eventually the hole will start to smoke. When it does, increase your speed in drawing the bow and press harder on the drill. Hot black powder will begin to fall into the tinder, and a spark will begin to glow. Transfer the faintly glowing tinder to your laid-out firewood. Keep gently fanning until it bursts into flame. What a feeling of accomplishment you will experience when you start your first fire without the aid of matches! It would be well to make an outfit now and practice until you become expert. I have gone into detail with several of these methods, for they may save your life.

FLINT AND STEEL

If you have no matches, or if you want to save them for an emergency, you may start a fire by using flint and steel. Look for a hard rock such as a piece of flint, quartz, agate, jasper, or any glassy stone. Gather dry tinder, *very* dry and very fine. With your hands close to the tinder, strike the flint with a knife blade or a piece of an old file, making a sharp, scraping downward motion so that your sparks will fall into the tinder. When the tinder begins smoldering a little, blow on it gently or fan it into a flame. Then place some fine kindling on your glowing or flaming tinder, or transport it to your fire layout.

Steel wool makes good tinder. It glows when sparks hit it; and when you touch a piece of paper to it, the paper will break into a bright flame immediately.

MAGNIFYING GLASS

If you should happen to have a magnifying glass, you can quickly and easily start a fire, provided there is sunshine. If you do not have a magnifying glass, use the lens from your flashlight, binoculars, camera, or the telescopic site from a gun. Focus the sunlight through the lens onto a small pile of fine tinder. Broken glass will give the same results but not as fast. Eskimos have used clear ice as a lens. They shave the ice to the form of a lens, smoothing it with the warmth of their hand and using it the same as you would a magnifying glass. There must be a hot sun, and your tinder must be very fine and very dry.

MAGIC MATCH

I keep Magic Match with me at all times wherever I go. You can purchase one at any sports store. It has to be scraped with a knife to form a small pile of powder which falls onto some very dry and fine tinder. Next scrape very fast with a sharp stroke until a spark ignites the powder, which in turn ignites the tinder. There are other types of artificial matches on the market which work equally as well.

CHAPTER 14

TYPES OF FIRES

SMALL FIRE

It will surprise you how a small fire can warm, for you can get close to it. Sit or kneel over it and drape your coat or blanket to direct the heat upward. You will find this much more effective than having a large fire with such intense heat that you cannot get close to it. The small fire takes much less fuel, also.

REFLECTOR FIRE

On the leeward side, drive two poles, leaning slightly away from the fire. Stack three or four logs against the two poles to reflect the heat. You may also use sod or boughs. The Eskimos have even used snow. The base of a tree or a large rock forms a natural reflector. If you find a cliff or large rock, sit or lie between the fire and the rock. This also holds true with a reflector fire built with logs.

STAR FIRE

When you have no ax or hatchet, a star fire is good to know about. Build a wigwam fire, described later. When it is burning well, add long poles or sticks, overlapping them in the center and radiating them out in a circle. As they burn, push them into the fire.

WARMED EARTH

Old-timers used to rake aside the evening campfire, which they built long and narrow and had burned down to a bed of coals. Then they would lie down on the warm ground and sleep comfortably through the coldest night.

FIRES FOR COOKING

WIGWAM FIRE

This type of fire is good for bringing water to a boil or cooking one kettle of food which does not require prolonged cooking. It is a hot fire and burns quickly. Start with tinder, and add kindling by stacking it up in wigwam fashion. Your fuel should consist of softwood, which burns rapidly and gives out a heat that quickly boils water.

HUNTER-TRAPPER FIRE

Select two green logs about four inches in diameter. Flatten one side of each, and lay the logs at an angle with the flat side up. Make the narrow end just wide enough to allow your smallest kettle to sit without falling. The wide end should be about a foot wide. Build a wigwam fire at the wide end, and feed it until you have a good bed of coals. If you want a hot fire, use softwood. If you want two fires, one for boiling water quickly and one for cooking something which requires a longer time, use hardwood to make a bed of coals, and rake them over to the narrow side. Then continue your first fire, switching to softwood. You may have to periodically replace your firedogs with fresh green sticks as they burn down.

CRISSCROSS FIRE

Make a layer of about five or six sticks of hardwood about two inches apart. Make another layer by laying the sticks crosswise. Continue this for several layers. Lay a small wigwam fire on top with good dry tinder and a few pitchy pieces of kindling. Let it burn down to your crisscross layers. When it burns down completely to the ground, you will have a large bed of coals for roasting food.

TRENCH FIRE

Dig a trench wider at the windward end and narrower at the leeward end. The trench should slant from ground level at the windward end to about eight to ten inches at the leeward end. Make the trench about twelve inches wide at the windward end and about six inches wide at the leeward or protected end. If you plan to use this trench for a while, line it with rocks. Make a fire toward the windward end to take advantage of the draft, and rake your coals toward the narrow end for cooking. Like the hunter-trapper, you can have a hot fire made with softwood at the wide end for boiling water or cooking one dish and have a bed of coals at the narrow end for prolonged cooking or roasting. This is a very versatile fire.

FIRE-IN-A-HOLE

Dig a small hole about ten inches deep and about a foot wide. Build a small fire in the bottom. For extra protection from the wind, pile on top of the leeward side the dirt removed from digging the hole. Place two or three green sticks across the top of the hole to support your kettle. The walls of the hole reflect the heat onto the kettle, thus requiring less fuel and smaller sticks. This is a good fire for a hot day or for windy weather. If you make the hole deep enough, you can cook vegetables in the coals by removing part of the coals and part of the hot rocks if you have lined it. Then place your food over the remaining coals in the hole. Pack the coals and hot rocks you removed in, around, and over the food. Pack about six inches of dirt over this, being sure that no steam escapes. In from three to six hours your vegetables will be done to a turn. If you have never done this before, you will have to take out a vegetable, the one which cooks the shortest time, and test it. Be sure when you put it back, in case it is not done enough, that you cover it well again and that there are no vents for steam to escape through. This fire provides a good way to cook corn, parsnips, potatoes, whole carrots, and whole onions. If you wish, wrap the vegetables in damp grass or non-tasting leaves, such as the grape or sycamore. If you have a Dutch oven, it makes an ideal container for your food.

STEW FIRE

This fire resembles the fire-in-a-hole or the trench fire. Dig a hole about two feet deep and about twelve inches in diameter. Build a fire in the bottom, using tinder and fine kindling and gradually adding softwood. When it is going well, add hardwood sticks about three feet long, poking them into the hole and filling up the hole as much as you can, yet leaving plenty of room for the circulation of air between the sticks. They will automatically feed the fire, dropping farther down into the hole as they burn. Next, firmly drive two poles into the ground on either side of the hole. Each pole should have a crotch or fork at the top. Lay a green stick across the two poles. Take another small stick with two notches on the same side, one at the top and one at the bottom. The upper notch will hook over the stick laid across the two poles, with your kettle hanging on the lower notch.

ALTAR FIRE

Use this fire when you know you will stay at your campsite over a long period of time, for it is built mainly for convenience, because it saves stooping to tend the fire. It is also a safe fire. Build the altar about two or three feet high from either logs or rocks, forming a hollow base. If using logs, fit them together by notching the ends log-cabin style. When you have the logs (or rocks) to the proper height, you will have a square hollow, which you should fill with nonflammable material such as sand or rocks up to about eight inches from the top. Build a wigwam fire of softwood to begin with, adding hardwood to make a bed of coals. Lay green sticks across the top of the altar to hold your kettle. A grate is preferable if you have one.

WAUGAN-STICK FIRE

This fire is also called tea-stick fire. It is about the simplest type of fire you can make for cooking. Select a hardwood green stick which does not burn readily. Avoid birch or ash, because they burn better when green. The stick should be springy, not stiff. Rest it upon a rock, and hold it down with another rock so that it curves upward. Build a wigwam fire of softwood under it. With a pothook, which I will describe later (see page 161), suspend a kettle over the fire. This is for fast boiling of water or for a dish which does not take long to cook. Another method of securing the stick is by driving a crotched stick into the ground and a few inches away driving another longer stick with a crotch. The first crotched stick will hold the long stick down, and the higher stick will support the long stick so that it will suspend over your fire. Make a notch in the long suspended stick over your fire on which to hang your kettle.

TRIPOD FIRE

Another simple cooking fire is the tripod fire. The Indians used this type of fire frequently for a quick meal. Interlock three hardwood sticks by the crotches on the top, or bind them with twine or a rawhide thong. Build a fire inside the base of the tripod. Use a pothook to suspend your kettle over the fire. You need not drive the sticks into the ground.

FIRE ON SNOW

It is also possible to build a fire on the snow. Look for dry firewood in a dense forest growth. Dead limbs are usually dry and are easily accessible, as they grow on the lower part of the trunk, protected by the thick foliage. Build an altar of crisscrossed green logs on top of the snow. This altar does not have to be as high as a regular fire. Make two layers of very green logs across the top, and build a fire over these layers. Replace the green logs as they burn down. If the outside of your fuel is wet, split the logs and use the inner part.

FIRE IN WET WEATHER

Scoop away wet, soggy ground. Build a small platform of stones, green sticks, or thick bark for a base. On this build a wigwam fire. Fuzz sticks are excellent to use in this situation. I will describe later how to make them. When your fire is burning well, lean wet wood against two poles, as in a reflector fire, so that they can dry out. If it is raining, build a windbreak and framework of sticks around and above the fire, using branches of evergreen.

FIRE AIDS

FUZZ STICKS

To make fuzz sticks, shave a straight-grained stick of dry softwood with single knife strokes until one end is a mass of wooden curls. Use them to start a fire.

TRENCH CANDLES

Make trench candles at home and take them with you when you go camping. Roll up several thicknesses of newspaper tightly, with a long piece of string inside to serve as a wick. Tie tightly with string, thus making log-like rolls. Soak the whole length in melted paraffin, and then cut it into sections of two or three inches. Let dry, and stack away in a box, ready to take with you. These make excellent kindling for starting your fire.

INSPIRATOR

Use a rubber hose or any hollow plant stem to blow on your fire. You can stick one end right into the wigwam fire center, thus fanning a glowing coal or glowing tinder into a flame.

CHAPTER 15

SHELTERS

GENERAL INFORMATION

Do not wait until darkness falls to provide a shelter. Start looking for a proper site at least two hours before sunset, depending upon how complicated a shelter you wish to make. Select a site where the sun can reach the shelter at least part of the day, preferably in the morning. In the summertime look for an area where breezes will help keep you cool and at the same time drive insects away. In the wintertime look for an area protected from wintry blasts. Avoid making your shelter under a large tree because of the danger of lightning, also because falling branches or drips of dew and rain may pester you.

Try to choose a site near good drinking water but not too near a large body of water such as a lake because of mosquitoes. Try to find a spot with enough level ground for your bed. Locate the site near material with which you can make your shelter and bed so that you will not have to haul in boughs, etc., from long distances. Situate it close to good firewood and drinking water.

Ravines or narrow valleys between steep hills tend to collect cold, heavy air at night. If you choose a higher elevation—a natural terrace or a large rock on the leeward side of a hill—you will find it several degrees warmer. The hill will serve as a windbreak.

The subject of shelters is very broad. I shall describe a few of the most practical types of shelters for a temporary stay in one location.

CAVES

You cannot depend on finding a cave for your shelter, but if you do find one, consider yourself very fortunate. Indians have used caves for centuries. Remember a few precautions, however. Caves form favorite dens for many wild animals, so beware of snakes or wild animals when you consider entering a cave. If it is large, be sure to take a candle with you to check its density of oxygen. At any rate, always take with you a flashlight or torch.

If the cave is small, you can easily heat it by a small fire at the entrance with a reflector of stacked green logs on the side of the fire away from the cave to reflect heat into the cave. Always beware of carbon monoxide poisoning.

TRENCH SHELTER

You can easily dig a trench if the soil is not too hard. The trench may be deep enough to stand upright in, but this is not necessary. Lay spruce or balsam boughs two feet thick on the floor of the trench, and a good thick covering of boughs on top of the trench. You may want to reserve one end of the floor without boughs to build a small wigwam fire for warmth. Leave a small open space right above your fire for the smoke to escape and to lessen the danger of carbon monoxide poisoning.

LEAN-TO SHELTER

Lash poles from saplings to small trees, to a large rock, or against a bank in the form of a lean-to. In some areas a fallen tree, if large enough in diameter, makes a good lean-to shelter. You can thatch your lean-to with evergreen boughs, starting at the bottom row and working up, overlapping the same as you would shingle a house. Other materials which you can use for thatching are palm or banana leaves, strips of bark, especially birch, bundles of long grass or hay bound closely together, or sod.

If you have nothing to lean poles against, drive two

upright poles into the ground until they are solid. The poles should be stiff, with crotches at the top. Place a cross pole in the crotches of the upright poles, and slantingly lay many sticks for the roof. Lash them to the cross pole with tough, long grasses, rope, or twine if you have it. About midway underneath the roof sticks or poles, lash another cross pole. Your lean-to is now ready for thatching. When finished, you will have a warm, snug temporary home. It protects best from the sun, wind, or cold weather but not too well when it rains. If used to protect from rain, thatch it with birch bark, or build it under a tree with very thick foliage. A reflector fire will adequately warm this type of shelter.

DESERT SHELTERS

Natural shelter is not easy to find in the desert. You may find it in the shade of cliffs, on the lee side of hills, or under the overhanging bank of a dry stream bed. In looking for a shelter in the desert, remember that not only does it get very hot in the daytime, but it can get very cold at night. To prepare for this, spread a blanket of desert vegetation over the ground while it is still hot. This prevents a rapid radiation of heat and will keep you warm during the cold night. Large Joshua trees, overhanging rocks, depressions, and large tumbled rocks broken off from the sides of a cliff may afford shelter from the sun. Sometimes you can find caves in desert areas. You can dig a trench and cover it for protection.

Remember that during the winter in certain parts of the desert the temperature can drop to freezing or below at night, and heavy rains do occur. A dry canyon is a dangerous place to make your camp because of the possibility of a cloudburst, which could cause sudden and violent floods to sweep along the valley.

SNOW SHELTERS

In snow country, your shelter serves primarily as a windbreak to help retain the heat from your fire and your body. Make your shelter small, windproof, and as nearly closed as possible. Be sure you build it at a right angle to the wind so that snowdrifts will not close the opening.

You may open a crude hole in deep snow from the top down. You could make it in the shape of a rough triangle, the roof and floor being the wider end, roofed and floored with evergreen, with the narrower part reflecting a small fire. You could also dig a trench in a low drift or bank of snow. Line the floor and roof with boughs the same as a dirt trench. Build a small altar fire on the bottom if the floor is covered with snow. Keep the fire small, and build a reflector to direct the heat toward the end of the trench which will contain your bed. Be sure to make your roof strong enough to hold a layer of snow. If you have no way to make a fire, cover your trench completely with boughs. You will get enough air to breathe, and if you keep your body away from direct contact with the snow, you will keep warm and snug.

There are two ways to build a snowhouse. One is to heap snow in a large mound, at least a little larger than you want your room. Pack down the final layer of snow. If the weather is quite a bit below freezing and you have water available, throw some over the mound to form a glaze. Otherwise just let the air harden it. Now you can burrow into the mound at right angles to the wind. Scoop out the snow until the walls are as thin as you feel feasible. Build a very small wigwam fire inside. When it has burned to coals, rake them out, poke a hole in the top of the dome, and allow your snowhouse to glaze inside. For warmth, you may keep a very small fire inside. This with your own body heat will keep you warm and snug. Be sure you have ample ventilation. It is better to have a slightly cold body than a dead one!

Another snowhouse is made by carving snow blocks cut from wind-hardened drifts. If the snow barely shows your footprints, it is just right to cut. Cut the blocks from twenty to thirty inches long and about a foot to a foot and a half wide. Place the first row of snow blocks in a circle. This will be your foundation. Slice the next snow blocks in a slant, and lay enough rows until you have made a rounded dome, completely enclosing your room. The last block at the top is a keystone. Patch the cracks with soft snow.

To keep out the fresh falling snow and cold air, you may build a long, low tunnel of snow blocks at your entrance. To make your room light, knock out a snow block in two or three places, replacing them with clear blocks of ice. You may also knock out a block near the top right over your very small wigwam fire. Be very, very careful to avoid carbon monoxide poisoning if you build a fire inside. You *must* have plenty of ventilation.

The tree-pit shelter is very easy to construct but can be made only in deep snow. Select a good evergreen tree with thick foliage and the lower limbs growing fairly close to the ground. Dig the snow away from around the trunk of the tree to the size you will need. Cover it over with boughs, also making a thick carpet of boughs under your feet. You can pile snow over your roof of boughs for additional insulation.

SHELTER BEDS

The purpose for a good bed in your shelter is two-fold: it will allow your body to relax more completely so that you can get a good night's sleep and awake in the morning refreshed, and it insulates your body from the chill of the ground or snow. It should be dry, smooth, and fairly soft. Remember that you will need more insulation beneath than above. Ground is a better conductor of heat than air. If you build your bed on top of the ground, build a fire a little while before time to retire. Let it burn down to coals. When ready to go to bed, rake them off and make your bed over the heated area.

Hard, level ground is more comfortable than soft, uneven ground. Avoid hummocks, slight depressions, sticks, and small stones when you choose the place to make your bed. Sand feels soft, but actually it is hard and will become uncomfortable if you sleep restlessly. If you have to lie on sand, scoop out hollows to fit the contours of your body, especially your hips.

BEDDING MATERIAL

You can make a good bed with dry grass; dry leaves; sedge (grasslike plants); boughs of evergreens, balsam, spruce, or hemlock; pine needles; moss; rushes; ferns; marsh hay; or animal skins.

BROWSE BED

Make a rectangular enclosure by securing with stakes four poles in the shape you wish your bed to be. Fill this form with pine needles, dry moss, leaves, ferns, or marsh hay.

A more luxurious or sophisticated browse bed can be made by placing a thick layer of resilient green boughs at the head of the bed within your form. Lay them with their underneath parts upward, opposite from the way they grow. Keep the butts well covered and pointing toward the bottom of the bed. Thatch the browse in this manner with row after row of boughs until it is a foot or more thick. Level it by poking in soft evergreen tips.

Making a browse bed is an art. You cannot do it by piling up an assortment of boughs in a haphazard fashion. Such a bed would be more uncomfortable than sleeping on the bare ground. Experience is the best teacher. After you have made a few browse beds, you will learn the art and become an expert. Balsam, hemlock, or spruce boughs seem to be the favorites with many in making a browse bed. It is best to collect only the lower boughs of these trees, for in this way the trees will not be injured.

STICK BED

Pioneers often made a stick bed. They staked down two parallel logs and laid springy sticks across them.

They next made a log frame, notched together log-cabin style, which they placed over the springy sticks, holding them in place. The space over the sticks was filled with some soft bedding material such as described in the preceding paragraphs.

FOUR-POSTER BED

Build a four-poster framework of poles about six inches from the ground. Lay small sticks across the frame, and cover with soft bedding material. This is very much like the stick bed, except it is off the ground a few inches and has four posters upon which you can hang your clothes. If you are in the tropics or where you can obtain bamboo, you can use bamboo for the frame. For bedding material, use long-leaf palm fronds. Split the leaves down the stem, lay the stems to the outside edge of the bed, and pile several layers deep.

CHAPTER 16

CAMP FURNISHINGS AND IMPROVISATIONS

ROLLTOP TABLE

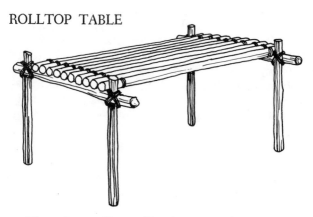

To make a rolltop table, drive into the ground four sturdy posts the size you wish your table to be. Lash securely two crosspieces—one at each end. Lash together sticks of uniform size and length to fit across the two crosspieces. If you have no twine, you can use tough grasses, vines, or anything of this nature you can find. This tabletop can be rolled for easy moving and used time and time again.

HEAVY, PERMANENT TABLE

Cut four heavy solid logs to form the four legs of your table as long as you wish the height of your table to be. Cut two logs to serve as braces at each end and nail to the table legs about ten to twelve inches from the ground. Cut a log to go lengthwise in the center be-

tween the two end braces to serve as another brace. Cut a log, split it in half, and nail the halves to the top of each of the two table legs, split side up. Cut several logs long enough to allow for a four- to six-inch overlap to serve as a tabletop. Split the logs, and notch them at each end to fit into the two top crosspieces. You will find this a very useful, sturdy table. See the illustration if you have any questions.

TEPEE TABLE

Lash four poles together like a tepee. Place small poles between the tepee poles to form a base for the table and also to serve as a brace. Fill in with poles across, making the tabletop. Lash securely. You can place a six- to eight-inch log, split side up, along each side to serve as a bench.

SLAB TABLE

This table is also a very heavy, permanent table. Select a large fallen tree, and cut a length the size of your table. Split it in half. Gouge out four holes to fit the legs into. Select four sturdy hardwood sticks to fit snugly into the four holes, to serve as table legs. With a little experimentation, you can make a solid table which you can use for years.

TRIPOD CHAIR

Make a tripod by lashing together securely three sturdy hardwood sticks. Lash them together at the approximate height you want the seat of your chair. Use a round flat rock for the seat, or a split, hewn piece of wood rounded to fit between the three sticks. Cut off the sticks flush with your chair seat. You can drive the three tripod sticks into the ground for greater security.

SLAB SEAT

Select a thick log, cut a two-foot length, and split it in two. This log should be well seasoned and not green. Cut a hardwood stick about two inches in diameter into four pieces long enough to serve as legs for your chair. Gouge out four holes as you did in making your slab table, and snugly fit the legs into the holes.

CHILD'S CHAIR

Select four sturdy hardwood sticks with crotches. Whittle each end like a stake. Lash together a rectangular frame. Pound the four hardwood sticks solidly into the ground. Attach a strip of canvas or other heavy cloth (you can use an animal skin) to the frame. Set the frame into the four crotches, and you have a cute and very comfortable chair.

LOG SEAT

Select a large log, and flatten it to form a bench seat. Cut notches on the underside of the seat to fit two other smaller logs which will serve as a base upon which the large log rests.

WASH-BASIN TRIPOD

Make a tripod the same as you did for your tripod chair, except you will want it much taller—at a height convenient for washing. Place a hollowed-out stone, birch-bark vessel, or basin on the top of your tripod.

COOLER

Make a rectangular frame of four sticks with cross-pieces where you want your shelves. Make it solid. You can make it as large as you wish. An average-size cooler is approximately eighteen inches square and about two to two and a half feet long. Make a solid top and bottom by lashing small sticks together. To make your shelves, lash sticks together, and attach inside the framework. Cover the frame with burlap, and nail into place. Place a receptacle of water on top (outside) with strips of burlap leading from the water-filled receptacle to all four sides of the frame. The water will travel down the burlap strips like wicks and wet the burlap sides. The cooler keeps the food cool by evaporation. Be sure to check the basin frequently and keep it filled with water. Generations of woodsmen have used this effective cooler. Other methods for keeping food cool are mentioned in the chapter on foods.

GREASE PIT

To make a grease pit for disposing of liquid waste, dig a hole on the downslope from camp, and line it with small stones or gravel. Cover it with a framework of small branches topped with dry leaves to act as filters as you pour dishwater or other liquid waste into it. Burn out the branches and leaves periodically. Replace them, and it is ready for use again. This grease pit is an important part of your camp setup to keep it clean, sweet, and sanitary. Throwing waste water on the ground attracts flies and other insects.

KITCHEN CABINET

It is difficult to describe how to make this useful piece of camp furniture. Be sure to closely examine the illustration when you have questions in your mind. Make a rolltop table as described earlier, only make the two back legs about two and a half feet longer than the front legs. Lash two cross poles, one near the top of the back legs and one about two or three inches above the tabletop. Lash these two cross poles to the back legs. Now make another roll top about half as long and not as wide as the large roll top. Lash one end of the tabletop to the upper cross poles, and place the other end in the crotches of two forked sticks. Check the illustration at this point.

CLAY OVEN

Getting the clay is the difficult task in making a clay oven. You may find a good cohesive clay along the banks of running streams or along the base of cliffs. To test it for cohesiveness and workability, allow it to dry out a little, knead it thoroughly, and curl it around your finger. If you can curl and uncurl it without its breaking or cracking, you can probably safely use it.

Dig enough clay for your oven, and be sure not to mix it with dirt. Let it dry for a while, then knead it and work it until it is pliable. You can add a little hay or grass to give it added body. Make a form of a bundle of sticks, just the size you want for the inside of your oven. Cover the outside of the bundle of sticks with clay about a foot thick, leaving a hole for the chimney and an opening in the front. Bake the clay in the sun for two or three days, then build a slow-burning fire of partly green wood inside, keeping it burning for two or three hours to bake the interior hard and firm. Be careful not to have too hot a fire inside, as it will crack your oven. To make a chimney, insert a small bundle of sticks into the chimney hole. Cover them with clay and bake as previously described. If cracks appear in your oven, all is not lost. Fill them with new clay and let them harden the next time you use the oven. When ready to bake, build a hot fire in the oven and keep it going until your oven becomes as hot as you want it. Experience will tell you. Then rake out the fire from the oven, place the food inside, and close the oven by fitting a tight door over the opening in the front. Use a flat stone, or you can make a door of green wood which does not burn readily. Place a flat stone over the chimney also.

This furnishes an excellent way to bake small loaves of bread, to cook vegetables, and to bake pies, cakes, or cookies. You can place your food on a flat rock. Be sure you wrap the vegetables in leaves, or keep them clean by some other method while baking.

POTHOOKS AND GIBS

A pothook is a small, short stick with a fork or crotch on one end and a notch cut in the other end which slants downward and is deep enough to hold the bail of a

kettle. Hook it onto the crosspiece of your two uprights driven into the ground, so that your kettle can hang directly over the fire. A gib is made by splicing two sticks together with their crotches or forks facing each other. One fork can be used to hold the bail of the kettle, the other fork to anchor the gib across a crosspiece of the two uprights as described above.

FIRE TONGS

Take a piece of hardwood such as hickory. About midway cut away part of the wood (not too much or it will be too thin) for about five or six inches, depending upon how long you want your tongs to be. This allows you to bend the stick. To keep it from springing back to its original shape, lash fiber, strong grass, rawhide, or twine around the tongs about halfway up. With these tongs you can pick up hot stones from your fire, or use them for any purpose you may think of.

STONE GRIDDLE

Find a large, flat, nonpopping rock. Place it on a platform of rocks or green logs. Build a fire underneath the stone, and another on top of the stone (after you have thoroughly scrubbed it). When the stone is sizzling hot, rake off the fire on top, clean the rock again, and fry your eggs or other food. Of course it works better if you can oil the top, but oil is hard to come by in the wilderness. Indians pressed oil from corn, nuts, and seeds, or used the fat from animals.

GREEN-STICK BROILER

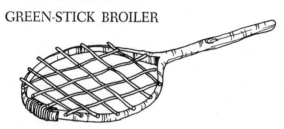

Gather a handful of green, sweet-tasting branches, and lace them together, weaving them under and over each other, making about one-half-inch squares. Split one end of a green willow stick. Lay the woven sticks across the split part of the willow stick, which has been lashed together after being rounded. It should look like a tennis racket when completed. See illustration.

COOKING FORK

Point the end of a sweet-tasting stick of fire-resistant wood. Split it down the middle at the point end to make two tines. Insert a small piece of wood at the artificial crotch to hold the tines apart. Then lash the fork just a little below the split to keep it from splitting too far. Use it to spear any large tubers such as potatoes, or in any way you would use a cooking fork.

LATRINE

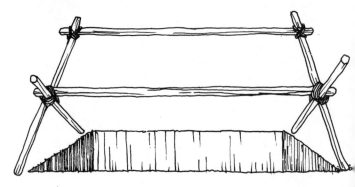

You should have a good latrine for your camp. Locate it away from your source of drinking water to avoid contamination. Situate it at least 100 feet from camp. Dig a trench about eighteen inches wide and two or three feet deep and long enough to accommodate one or two people, as you wish. If you plan to camp there for some time, you may want to dig it deeper. Save the dirt, piling it near the trench so that you can shovel some dirt into the trench after each use.

A good latrine should have a cleared path leading to it, making it safe to get to at night. A thick screen of brush will hide it from view, or you may locate it down over a little hill, out of sight of the camp. If no brush is available, you can make a framework around it with a lattice of sticks. It can be thatched with evergreen boughs for greater privacy.

For a seat, drive two sets of poles into the ground at angles and lash them together. The poles at the back should be longer than at the front. Lay a smooth-bark pole across the two artificial crotches to form the seat.

Another pole can be lashed to the back poles a little less than shoulder height for a backrest. See illustration.

For a permanent and more comfortable seat, split a large log and hew a slab about two or three inches thick. Cut out one or two holes from eight to ten inches in diameter. Set the slab on logs at the height you desire, or you can use large rocks for the base. Cover the holes with a slab of wood or a flat stone after using the latrine. If you cover with dirt after each use, there will be little or no odor. You can also use ashes. Burn out your latrine periodically if you do not cover it with dirt each time. When the trench is full, cover with dirt or ashes and dig a new trench nearby. Set up a washbasin tripod nearby for hand washing.

CHAPTER 17

SURVIVAL IN WINTER OR COLD COUNTRY

It is difficult enough to survive in the wilderness in the spring and summer months, or even in autumn weather. But it is quite another thing to find yourself isolated in the north country or anywhere in the cold winter months. You should know several pointers that will make your chances for survival in cold climes much greater.

GENERAL INFORMATION

Your main concern in cold or freezing weather is to keep dry. Avoid overexertion, because it will cause you to perspire. Sweat will freeze inside your clothing, and the ice will decrease the effect of insulation and increase the chance of freezing. Keep your hands and feet dry. Avoid sleeping on bare ground.

When you work in freezing weather, open your clothes at the neck and wrists and loosen them at the waist. In other words, wear your clothes loosely. A tight fit cuts off circulation and increases danger of freezing. Take off any excess clothing while working, and put them on again when finished. Do not sleep in clothes worn during the day if perspiration has dampened them. You must wear dry clothing day and night.

Avoid snow blindness, and guard against frostbite. Keep snow out of your boots (or shoes) and gloves. Brush the snow from your clothes before entering your shelter or going near your fire. Keep out of the wind. Dry wet clothing and socks before your fire. Drink plenty of water. This helps your kidneys function well and will help eliminate constipation difficulties. The kidneys must do most of the elimination of wastes that perspiration usually cares for in warm weather.

Paradoxically, temperatures are often warmer below the snow than above it. Remember that any windbreak will help preserve body heat. Generally, hollows and valleys are colder than protected slopes and ridges. Temperatures usually rise during a blizzard or snowstorm. Remember that plenty of rest and food is important in cold country. Never travel until you are completely exhausted, but take frequent rests, and sleep when you feel like it. Many people have the idea that if they sleep, they will surely freeze to death. Unless you are exhausted, the cold will wake you up before you freeze. For temporary rest and protection, dig into the snow with your back to the wind, and pull your arms out of your sleeves, holding them against your body for warmth.

Do not sit directly on the snow if you can place something under you. If you get wet in extremely cold weather, make a fire immediately in the most sheltered spot you can find, and dry out. Without a fire, keep moving until your body heat has warmed and dried your inner garments. Breathe only through your nose. This warms the air before it reaches your lungs, thus reducing the danger of frosting them. Try to get something hot inside you. Choose a campsite near water but on high, dry ground. Stay away from thick woods. Choose a ridgetop, lakeshore, or some other spot that gets an onshore breeze.

FIRE FOR WARMTH

In building a fire in snow country, do not start it under a snow-covered tree. Snow may fall and put out the fire. Look for any woody brush or shrub, and burn roots as well as stems. If you can find pitchy wood such as a knot or stump, cut it up fine for kindling. Fine slivers of pitchy wood make excellent tinder. You can find dry wood on the underside of trees with thick foliage, in hollow trees or logs, under overhanging rocks, or in caves. If you cannot find any dry wood in any of these areas, split wet wood and use the inner part. It will be dry, as rain does not soak very far into the wood, especially if you get your wood from a leaning dead tree. After you get your fire started, even very wet wood will burn quite well. Make a reflector, and stack your wet wood near your fire so that it can dry out while your fire is burning.

Other good material to burn is spruce, which burns very well when green, dried lichens, moss, heather, scrub willow, alders, and driftwood. Loose bark from birch trees contains resinous oils and ignites easily and burns fiercely. If there is snow on the ground, build an altar fire of green logs or rocks as described in the chapter on types of fires.

WATER

If snow covers the ground and you are near an ice-covered stream or lake, remember that melted ice will yield more water than melted snow. You will get more water in less time, and it will take less heat. If you are on the ocean, old sea ice is better for drinking water than new ice. Old sea ice is bluish and has rounded corners. It is free from salt. New ice is gray, milky, and hard. It is salty. Do not drink from new ice.

In cold weather you will find that springs and spring-fed streams will not freeze over as soon as other water-courses. Eating snow and ice may quench your thirst, but it will chill your stomach and reduce your body temperature. Always heat it at least long enough to take the chill off. If possible, drink two pints of hot water daily.

FOOD

Food is hard to find when snow covers the ground. Roots and berries will be available under the snow if you know just where to look for them. If you observe the feeding habits of birds and small animals, you may locate the burrows of mice and lemmings. They will have roots and other edible foods in them. Muskrat houses are found in low mounds in swamps and shallow lakes. They will also contain edible roots.

The inner bark of roots and stems of willow, spruce, alder, hemlock, basswood, and birch are all edible. First peel off the soft inner bark, and then cut it into narrow strips. You may either eat it fresh or dry it in the sun. Do not overlook this important source of food. Lichens (reindeer moss) are rich in carbohydrates even though they are not very tasty and may taste quite bitter. However, they are not poisonous. Do not eat them raw. Crumble them in water, let them soak for several hours, then boil them until they are reduced to a jellylike substance. They are now ready to eat. Some people cook them, then dry them until they are brittle. They grind them to powder, put them in a tight container, and boil when needed.

Emergency Rescue Survival, Air Force Manual claims that mushrooms on the tundra in arctic and subarctic regions are not poisonous, but they are few and far between. The buds of basswood, poplar, and maple and the shoots of spruce and tamarack are edible. The leaves of mountain sorrel, young willows, and fireweed can be boiled and eaten.

SHELTER

You can dig a trench in the snow, and floor and roof it with evergreen boughs. If your roof is strong enough, pack a layer of snow on top for further protection and insulation. Leave a small hole in the top for smoke to escape. Build a very small fire on a low altar of green logs at one end of the trench. You do not need a large fire. Be *sure* you have good ventilation while your fire is burning. You are indeed fortunate if you can find a cave or a deep overhanging rock for protection. If the snow is not deep enough to dig a trench, make a lean-to shelter.

FROSTBITE

Excessive loss of heat from any part of the body restricts circulation, making the extremities subject to frostbite. If you are with another person, watch each other for signs of frostbite—white spots on face and ears. Some people rub the affected area with snow. This only makes the area colder and worsens the condition. You may also break down frozen tissues by rubbing. Keep the affected part away from the fire. Quick thawing results in inflammation and possible gangrene. Apply cold water (not ice water) compresses to gradually raise the temperature. If the frostbite is blackened and the flesh begins to peel, treat it as a burn. If you feel you are in danger of freezing, keep moving, get to warmth as quickly as possible, and get something hot to drink. Do *not* drink alcoholic beverages.

SNOW BLINDNESS

Many people become snow-blind if their eyes are exposed to intense sunlight upon the snow for an extended period of time. It may range from a slight eye irritation to temporary blindness for several days. The first indication is a feeling that you have sand in your eyes. Your eyes may become bloodshot, or you may have a copious flow of tears and perhaps even a discharge from the eyes. Wash your eyes with cool, boiled water. Apply cold compresses. If you become blinded, wear a dark bandage over your eyes.

Prevention of snow blindness is very simple. Travel at night, if possible, or make yourself sunglasses out of a piece of wood, leather, or other material. Make narrow slits in the material for your eyes. Dark glasses are best if you have them. You might get a severe headache due to excessive glare, but this is to be expected.

SIMPLE SLED FOR HAULING

The sled I shall describe is about as simple as you can make. It merely consists of a large limb which has a crotch. Cut off the two branches the length you want the bed of your sled. Either lash or nail smaller crosspieces (branches) to the two larger branches, which serve as runners. Cut off the trunk to the desired length, and with a piece of rawhide or rope lash it in a notch to hold it securely. This serves as a draw rope. You will be surprised at the heavy load this simple yet sturdy sled can carry.

SNOWSHOES

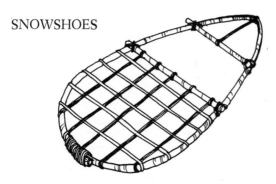

Very simple snowshoes can be made from materials close at hand if you find it necessary to go on foot for some distance. Any green flexible wood will do for the frame, but some think ash and hickory are the best. If you place the wood in hot water, it will become more flexible. Gradually bend the frame into shape until it resembles a bear's paw. Lash the large end (the top) together. Whittle or scoop out the narrow end. (See illustration.) Lash a crosspiece of wood about three or four inches from the narrow end. Lash some rawhide from the middle of the crosspiece to the middle of the narrow end of the frame. Place another crosspiece about three inches from the first crosspiece toward the larger end. Make notches in your frame to hold the rawhide lashing more securely. Keep lashing rawhide (basswood bark can be used) every inch or so across the frame. Weave rawhide from the rounded end (the large end) of the frame to the second crosspiece. Be sure to observe the illustration as you proceed.

Reserve two pieces of rawhide for tying around the toe securely. The heel must be loose. You should practice making a few at home now so that, when you find yourself in the wilderness, you will be able to go right ahead and make a good snowshoe. As I mentioned earlier, if you do not have rawhide, you can use basswood bark or anything flexible enough to serve as lash material. Oval-shaped snowshoes are best for wooded, hilly country, but a long, tapering shape is best when the snow is light and dry.

WALKING ON SNOWSHOES

When walking on snowshoes, you will have to learn to raise your heel quite high. Lift it just high enough to clear the top of the snow. You will have to learn by experience just how far apart to hold your feet when walking. Bring your rear snowshoe forward and outward far enough so you will not strike the ankle of the other foot as it passes. This takes practice.

PRECAUTIONS WITH SNOWSHOES

Never try to bridge a gap with your snowshoes. Do not jump. You might land on a buried rock or stump which could cause you to injure your foot or perhaps sprain your ankle. A snowshoe is not a ski. If you try to ski downhill in snowshoes, you may very well ruin your webbing. It is best to wear medium-high, soft-soled heavy moccasins if you have a pair.

CHAPTER 18

SURVIVAL IN THE DESERT
OR IN HOT WEATHER

Although the desert poses a formidable threat for most people, Arabs and others have lived in desert areas for centuries and actually enjoy life. The important difference between them and us is that they have accustomed themselves to their environment. Now if we should find ourselves stranded in the desert, we would have to adjust quickly, using good judgment and wisdom if we want to survive.

GENERAL INFORMATION

Shelter from the sun and heat is one of your greatest concerns in the desert. First search for shade. We will hope that you have a fair supply of water with you. You may find natural shade in a rock ledge, the wall of a dry stream, or, fortunately, a cave.

Do not travel during the day if the weather is extremely hot. Travel at night. During the day rest in any available shade. If a dust storm comes up, turn your back to it and cover your nose with a handkerchief. Slow motion is the watchword in the desert. Desert nomads are not lazy. They have simply learned to live at the slow pace they have found necessary for survival. If you move slowly, you will conserve your strength and will require less water intake. Do not sit directly on the hot desert sand if you can sit even a few inches off the ground. It is thirty degrees cooler one foot from the ground than it is directly on the ground—a difference that could mean your survival.

CLOTHING

Contrary to general belief, it is best to keep your clothes on in hot weather. Wear a hat, shoes or sandals, long-sleeved shirt or blouse, and men should wear long pants. However, wear your clothes loosely. Clothing and shoes will protect you from the sun, heat, sunburn, sand, and insects. It is important to control sweating. Wearing clothing will cause perspiration to evaporate slowly. Taking your clothes off only causes you to perspire more freely and rapidly, thus increasing the hazard of sunburn. Wear a neckpiece, if possible, to protect the back of your neck. Light-colored clothing reflects the heat of the sun and keeps out hot desert air. If you do not have sunglasses, make an improvisation as described in the chapter on survival in cold country.

THE DESERT IN WINTER

Winter months in the desert can produce freezing temperatures. This is especially true at night. Build a small fire to avoid getting chilled. It is entirely possible for deserts to have heavy rains in winter. Therefore, avoid making your camp in a dry canyon, for a sudden cloudburst may produce violent flash floods which could sweep you down the canyon in a roaring wall of water.

WATER

In the desert your life depends upon your ability to find water. You may be fortunate enough to have a small supply with you, but you will eventually have to find water. You will need a minimum of four quarts a day if the weather is extremely hot. If you travel by night, you will be able to travel about twenty miles on those four quarts. But if you travel by day, you will have to reduce your mileage to less than half.

If you have a good water source, drink more and drink more frequently than you think you should if you want to keep in good health. In trying to find water in the desert, look for dry stream beds if you are in very stony, desert country. Dig at the lowest point on the greater curvature of a bend in the stream channel. If you are in the sand dunes, look for water between the outermost dunes rather than in the middle of them. Pick the lowest point between the dunes and dig deep, from three to six feet. If you hit damp sand, keep digging until you strike water.

Desert lakes are usually salty, so, for fresh water, dig a hole in the depression behind the sand dune nearest the lake. As soon as you hit wet sand, stop digging. Wait until the water seeps in. This water will be fresh or nearly so. If you had kept on digging, you would in all probability have hit salt water.

It is possible to collect dew. Dig a hole, and line it with canvas or plastic. Then dig out rocks from at least one foot underground, and fill the plastic-lined hole. Collect your dew early in the morning. You will discover that during the night and early dawn, dew has collected on the rocks and has run down into your plastic. If you make several of these holes, you will be surprised how much dew you can collect. You can also mop up dew with a cloth from plants or rocks containing slight depressions.

Cactus plants usually contain water. However, do not drink from any cactus plant or any plant which looks like a cactus plant which has a milky sap. Any succulent, fleshy plant will contain water. The prickly pear not only is nutritious but also helps quench thirst. The pads (leaves) and stems roasted will also quench your thirst.

The barrel cactus provides an excellent source of water. Cut or hack off the top and mash down the pulp against the walls of the plant. The bowl of the cactus will fill up with water which oozes out of the inside walls of the plant. Then you can scoop the water up in your hand. Or, if you have a larger container to receive the water, cut a hole a few inches from the bottom of the plant and let the water pour out into your container. Do not do this unless there are several in your party, as this water does not keep very well.

Watch the actions of birds and animals. If you hear a bird chirping, you can almost be sure that water is near. A flock of circling birds sometimes denotes water. Watch for runways and trails of animals. In the desert, every little clue which may lead to water may make the difference between life and death.

FOOD

You can be sure that the desert is not a supermarket for food. However, there is food if you exert the energy and time to find it. Desert plants are one source of food. They may look hopelessly dry, but the soft parts of desert plants which grow above the ground are usually edible, such as the flowers, fruit, seeds, and young shoots. Of course, succulent or fleshy, thick plants offer the best source of both food and water. Dig to find the roots of trees and shrubs. Peel off the root bark. The soft inner bark is usually edible, and you may drink the water which will drip from the cut root surface.

Mesquite or honeypod (*Prosopis glandulosa*), a small tree or shrub found in dry desert regions, has pods resembling string beans. They are a bright lemon-yellow when ripe and have a sweet, juicy pulp surrounding hard seeds. You can eat the beans raw or dry them for future use. Soak them to remove the bitterness before cooking. Some Indians gathered the green pods and cooked them like string beans or any other green vegetable. Most of the time, however, they ground the dried pods into a meal, formed them into patties, and baked them in coals or hot ashes.

The screw bean (*Prosopis pubescens*) is a small desert tree or shrub which looks very much like the mesquite. However, the pods are in clusters about two inches long and look like tightly twisted cylinders. Like the mesquite, the pods are sweet. They contain even a higher amount of sugar, hence they are very nutritious. You may grind or pound the dried pods into a meal and bake them in little cakes. Some Indian tribes boiled the pods and made a molasseslike syrup from them.

Although food is scarce in the desert, remember that you can survive for days, and even weeks, providing you have an ample supply of water, so don't panic.

MAKING A FIRE IN THE DESERT

Cooking fires cannot be large in any desert because fuel is scarce. Utilize everything available which will serve as fuel—twigs, leaves, stems, roots. If you come across an old unused desert trail, you are likely to find animal dung, which, if dry, will give off a very hot flame. Even jackrabbit pellets will burn. Do not overlook anything that will burn.

FIRST AID IN THE DESERT

Exposure to the sun and heat will constitute your greatest health hazard. *Heat cramps* may occur in the legs or abdominal muscles. If you have this condition, you must rest. If you have salt and water with you, dissolve one-half teaspoon of salt to a half cup of water and take a half cup every fifteen minutes for four doses. Massage the affected legs, though not too vigorously, and apply warm wet cloths. This usually gives relief. Heat cramps are due to loss of chemicals in profuse perspiration and may be associated with heat exhaustion.

Certain symptoms indicate *heat exhaustion*. In a mild case you will feel tired and have a headache and nausea. In more severe cases you will have profuse perspiration, extreme weakness, and your skin will turn pale and clammy. You may vomit. Again, rest is essential. Take salt water as prescribed for heat cramps. Hunt for a shady spot.

Your first symptom of *heat stroke* is likely to be a headache. You will have hot, dry skin and a strong, rapid pulse. You may feel dizzy and become nauseated. Your face will be red. You will not sweat. It is imperative that you find shade and get into it immediately. Loosen your clothing, and lie flat on the ground. Saturate your clothes with water and fan yourself. You must cool down your body or you may lapse into unconsciousness. Do not take any stimulants. Make a salt solution (a half teaspoon of salt to a half cup of water) and take a half cup—a sip at a time—every fifteen minutes for four doses. Heat stroke can be very serious. It is important to get out of the desert as fast as possible and seek medical help if one of your party becomes unconscious.

Chapter 19

OUTDOOR SANITATION AND HEALTH

The subject of health and sanitation is very important in wilderness living. You will be far from skilled medical help, and you will not have a drugstore close at hand. A few simple rules might help you keep in good health and have a sweet, clean, wholesome environment.

PURE WATER SUPPLY

One of the important concerns about a wilderness camp is a safe water supply. Never go by appearances, thinking that clear, sparkling water must be pure and safe. It can be badly contaminated. On the other hand, I have seen brown, evil-smelling water which, when tested, proved safe. Contamination of water may be in the form of bacteria, such as typhoid or *Escherichia coli* (which usually denotes the presence of human wastes). A beautiful stream may appear pure, sweet, and entirely safe, yet a little investigation may reveal the half-decayed body of an animal or bird just a little distance upstream. If there is any doubt in your mind about the safety of an available source of water supply, boil the water for thirty minutes. Remember that springs on forested hillsides are usually safe.

GARBAGE

Bury all garbage. You may use the garbage pit as described in the chapter on camp improvisations, but always burn it out periodically. Remember that some prowling animal may dig up the garbage if it is buried too shallow. As mentioned before, get used to using a grease pit for dishwater and liquid slops. Burn out the pit periodically. Carry bits of fruit and vegetables, which make good food for wild animals, well away from your camp or shelter. Dry other solid wastes until they will burn in a brisk fire.

HUMAN WASTES

You should make your latrine well away from camp and downhill at least one hundred feet. Locate it so that it will not seep into your water source. For a temporary latrine, you may dig a trench two to three feet deep and pile dirt along the sides so that it can easily be covered after each use. After using it for several days, burn a fire over it. You may provide privacy by building a screen of boughs around it; however, it is best to locate it near a natural screen of bushes or underbrush. The Bible has given us a record of the careful sanitation laws given to the children of Israel. Concerning human wastes we read in Deuteronomy 23:13, 14, "And thou shalt have a paddle [the margin reads, "shovel"] upon thy weapon; and it shall be, when thou wilt ease thyself abroad, thou shalt dig therewith, and shalt turn back and cover that which cometh from thee: for the Lord thy God walketh in the midst of thy camp; . . . therefore shall thy camp be holy: that he see no unclean thing in thee."

THE DAILY BATH

Keep yourself and your clothing clean. A daily sponge bath or a dip in a nearby stream is necessary for good health. The book *Life at Its Best,* by Ellen G. White, page 71, stresses the importance of the daily bath:

"Scrupulous cleanliness is essential to both physical and mental health. Impurities are constantly thrown off from the body through the skin. Its millions of pores are quickly clogged unless kept clean by frequent bathing, and the impurities which should pass off through the skin become an additional burden to the other eliminating organs. . . .

"A bath, properly taken, fortifies against cold, because it improves the circulation; the blood is brought to the surface, and a more easy and regular flow is obtained. The mind and the body are alike invigorated. The muscles become more flexible, the intellect is made brighter. . . . Bathing helps the bowels, the stomach, and the liver, giving health and energy to each, and it promotes digestion."

It is a real temptation in the wilderness to neglect taking a daily bath. It may be cold, and you may have to heat water on an open wood fire. Yes, it is inconvenient, yet how important!

WASHING YOUR CLOTHING

Wash your clothes frequently. If you do not have regular soap, remember that the Indians used the blossoms of mountain lilac (*Ceanothus integerrimus, parvifolius*) or yucca and Joshua tree (*Cleistoyucca abornescens*) stems made into a pulp to substitute for soap. It worked very well. They still wash their hair with these natural soaps. Indian soaproot (*Chlorogalum pomeridianum*) bulbs are very lathery and have been used for years by the Indians to wash their clothes and hair.

Notice the following quotation concerning the washing of your clothes:

"It is important also that the clothing be kept clean. The garments worn absorb the waste matter that passes off through the pores; if they are not frequently changed and washed, the impurities will be reabsorbed.

"Every form of uncleanliness tends to disease. Death-producing germs abound in dark, neglected corners, in decaying refuse, in dampness and mold and must. No waste vegetables or heaps of fallen leaves should be allowed to remain near the house [in your case, camp], to decay and poison the air."—*Ibid.*, pp. 71, 72. So we see from this statement that it is important after taking a bath not to put on the same soiled clothing.

Do not eat half-spoiled fruit or vegetables. A sentence

taken from the book *Counsels on Diet and Foods,* by Ellen G. White, page 309, states, "More die by eating decayed fruit and decayed vegetables which ferment in the stomach and result in blood poisoning, than we have any idea of." We should boil our utensils periodically to kill germs.

DIARRHEA

If a member of your group gets diarrhea, carefully observe personal cleanliness. Washing the hands with soap and water is most important. Boil dishes and tableware. Dispose of human waste carefully. The afflicted person should rest a great deal and fast for twenty-four hours, but drink boiled water during the fast. Then he should take only liquid foods for a day or two. He should avoid sugars and starches.

CONSTIPATION

Many times the only reason for constipation is the lack of enough fluid intake. Some people simply do not drink enough water. The afflicted person should drink quantities of water. He should eat fresh or dried fruit, vegetables with roughage, and not eat too heavily of starchy foods. Nature has several very fine laxatives. The bark from stems of cascara sagrada, sometimes called buckthorn (*Rhamnus purshiana*), can be steeped in boiling water. Start out cautiously so as not to take an overdose. People differ as to the amount they can take. Increase the dosage as the need arises. You can also peel off birch bark and steep a handful in hot water for a laxative. Senna leaves (*Cassia angustifolia, acutifolia*) can also be steeped in hot water and taken, but be careful, for this can produce griping effects. A lack of exercise coupled with not enough fluid intake frequently results in mild constipation.

Indians centuries ago gave enemas by using a small hollow bone from an animal or fowl as an enema tip. They secured it to a short section of intestines from an animal and lashed it securely to the stomach or bladder of a freshly killed animal or to a vessel made from an animal skin.

FATIGUE

Another health hazard in the wilderness is severe fatigue. Try to save your strength as much as possible, and avoid becoming exhausted. Try to get at least eight hours of sleep every night. Lie down during the day and try to relax completely, especially if you work at hard physical labor or on some project such as building a simple log cabin for a more or less permanent shelter. If you do hard work, rest ten minutes each working hour. You will get more done in the long run, and you will endure longer. The danger in this area comes from the fact that most of us are soft. We have had too many modern conveniences, haven't walked enough, and have not done hard physical labor—now all of a sudden we find ourselves in a wilderness situation demanding very hard work. Some of you may have a heart condition which you will have to watch.

AVOID CATCHING A COLD

It is dangerous to catch a cold in the wilderness. You are far from a doctor or from a drugstore where you can purchase cold remedies. Avoid getting chilled. If your clothes get wet, dry them if at all possible. A cold can quickly develop into pneumonia in the wilderness, especially if you do not get sufficient vitamin C. Rose hips (*Rosa californica* and others) are very high in vitamin C. Cut the rose hip in two, pry out the seeds, and eat the bright orange or red shell. The leaves of the stinging nettle (*Urtica dioica*) also contain much vitamin C. Gather the leaves carefully, and boil like spinach. The nettles melt, and it is really a very tasty dish. I imagine that citrus fruits such as oranges, lemons, grapefruits, and limes will not be available in the wilderness unless you find yourself in a tropical region.

CHAPTER 20

WILDERNESS FIRST AID

When in the wilderness, you are miles from a doctor. Accidents and illnesses will arise, and you will need to care for yourself the best you know how. Take a course in standard and advance first aid from the Red Cross *now* so that, when the need arises, you will have the knowledge that may save your own life or the life of a loved one.

WOUNDS

There are four kinds of wounds:

1. Abrasions, including scuffs, scrapes, and friction burns gotten perhaps from skidding along a rocky wilderness trail.

2. Incised (cut) wounds—sharp cuts that bleed freely. They may result from stepping on a razor-sharp obsidian stone.

3. Lacerated wounds, made by being struck by something blunt which makes a jagged tear in the flesh.

4. Puncture wounds made by a thorn, a sharp stick, a sliver of a sharp stone, or anything else that makes a wound similar to one made by a nail or ice pick.

BLEEDING

Pressure directly over a wound usually stops the bleeding until you can get something to wrap tightly around the wound. The brachial artery, a pressure point that can be used if bleeding occurs in the arm below the point of pressure, is on the inner side of the arm halfway between the elbow and the armpit. The femoral artery is a pressure point just below the groin on the front, inner part of the thigh. Pressure on this point takes care of bleeding in the leg below the point of pressure.

Use the tourniquet only as a last resort when other efforts do not stop the bleeding, and use it only when severe bleeding involves an extremity in which large arteries are severed, or in cases of partial or complete severance of a body part. If you do apply a tourniquet, do not leave it on indefinitely. The old method of loosening the tourniquet every fifteen minutes is not used now, for the tourniquet can be kept in place for one or two hours without causing further damage to the extremity.

SHOCK

Treat a severely injured person for shock. The symptoms of shock usually develop gradually and so may not be noticeable at first. Shock is a depressed condition of many of the body functions due to failure of enough blood to circulate through the body. It follows serious injury, or extreme fright, or even witnessing or going through some horrible experience.

The following are symptoms of shock: The skin becomes pale, cold, moist, and clammy. The eyes may look vacant, without luster, and have dilated pupils. The breathing usually is shallow and irregular, and there may be symptoms of air hunger (gasping for air). Sometimes nausea, faintness, or even unconsciousness may develop. The pulse will be weak, irregular, rapid, or even absent in extreme cases.

To treat for shock, keep the person lying flat. Raise the legs twelve to eighteen inches, unless the head is injured or the chest punctured. Keep him warm, but only enough to prevent shivering. You may help him conserve heat by placing a blanket under him. Do not add heat. Simply try to prevent a large loss of body heat. If you have no blanket, build a fire, later rake it to one side, and drag him onto the warm ground.

Fluids have value in shock, but do not give them if the person is unconscious, partly conscious, nauseated, or has a penetrating abdominal wound. Plain water, neither hot nor cold, is the best fluid. Stimulants have no value in traumatic shock.

BURNS

In first-degree burns the skin is reddened. In second-degree burns the skin is blistered, painful, and swollen. Third-degree burns are the most serious, because the burn goes through the skin into the deeper tissues. Remember four points when dealing with burns:

1. Treat for shock as described in preceding paragraphs.

2. Relieve pain by excluding air from the burn.

3. In first- and second-degree burns, apply very cold water.

4. Prevent contamination. Cover the burn with the cleanest cloth you have. If in the wilderness, take a flaming stick and slightly scorch the cloth and apply immediately without touching the side which will cover the burned area. Do not break blisters. There is too much danger of contamination.

A severely burned person needs fluids, but they often cause nausea. If you are fortunate enough to have a first-aid kit with you in the wilderness, begin giving at fifteen-minute intervals half-glass doses of a solution made by dissolving one-half level teaspoon salt and one-half level teaspoon baking soda in a quart of water. In mild acid burns, wash the wound freely with lots of water, and apply baking soda if you have it. In alkali burns, wash the wound in large quantities of water.

DROWNING

You must be careful when attempting to rescue a drowning person that you do not endanger your own life. He may grip you and drag you underwater, because he has extra strength and is usually panicky. Extend to him a hand, a foot, your shirt, a branch, or pole, and pull him to safety. If he is out too far to reach from the bank, wade in chest deep and extend something to him and pull him in. If he is not breathing when rescued, turn him on his stomach and raise him up with both hands on his waist. Turn his head to one side so that the water will run out; otherwise it will stay in his mouth, and he may choke. Use mouth-to-mouth resuscitation or the pressure arm-lift method.

SNAKEBITE

There are three pit vipers in the United States—the rattlesnake, the copperhead, and the cottonmouth (water moccasin). There is one other poisonous snake—the coral snake. These are the four most common. There is immediate pain after viper venom is injected. The poisoned part soon swells and becomes discolored. Coral snake venom causes only a slight burning pain and a mild swelling at the site of the wound. Pit vipers may introduce germs as well as venom. When snake venom is deposited, there is general weakness, shortness of breath, nausea, vomiting, a weak and rapid pulse, and occasionally dimness of vision. The person bitten may become unconscious.

Have the person stop all activities AT ONCE. Remember the words TIE, CUT, SUCK:

1. Tie a constricting band *above* the bite if it is on an arm or a leg. There should be some oozing from the wound.

2. Sterilize a knife blade with a match flame or a small flaming stick, and make cuts. Try to get into the venom deposit points. Remember that the snake strikes downward, and that the fangs retract. Crosscuts one-fourth inch long may be made at each fang mark. Longitudinal cuts may be deeper because muscles and nerves run in a longitudinal direction. Be careful not to sever them.

3. Apply suction by using your mouth, or, if you

happen to have a snakebite kit, use the suction cups. If you have an open sore in your mouth, let someone else apply the suction. Continue suction for an hour or more. Keep the person lying down with the injured part a little lower than the rest of the body. If it is possible to apply cold to the involved part, this treatment measure would give relief from pain and might slow down absorption of poison into the system. Try to find a quiet stream in a shaded area in which you might wring out a cloth. The water here would be cold enough to be effective.

FRACTURES

Of the several kinds of breaks in bones, the most common is the simple fracture, in which there is no open wound and therefore no danger of infection. The compound fracture involves an open wound. The broken bone may or may not protrude through the skin, and there may be severe bleeding. The person may feel or hear the bone snap and afterward hear or feel a grating together of the bone parts. The person will suffer pain and tenderness at the site of any break. The fractured part may swell and become deformed and discolored. A person *can* move a broken bone, contrary to common belief. Often he can move the parts below the break with little or no distress.

If the bone protrudes from the skin, do not push it back in if you think you can get to a doctor soon. If no hope of getting help is in sight, splinting and traction may be necessary. The bone will slip back by itself when the limb is straightened for splinting. Keep the broken ends and adjacent joints quiet. Treat for shock. Apply as clean a dressing as it is possible to obtain. If you cannot apply traction, apply a splint to each side of the fracture if it is of the leg or arm. If you are in the woods, you will probably be able to find sticks to use for this purpose. You can always use the "well-leg" splint, splinting the injured leg to the well leg by lashing them together with long strands of tough grass or anything you can find. You may have to rip up your shirt or a petticoat.

Space does not permit a detailed explanation of the treatment for each kind of fracture, such as skull, jaw-bone, collarbone, ribs, and other types. Learn that from a Red Cross course in first aid *now*.

IMPROVISED STRETCHER

Cut two poles, and lash boughs across, rather close together, somewhat like a ladder. Lay the injured person on this ladderlike improvisation, and carry him gently, with as little swaying motion as possible, to the desired destination.

Injuries in the wilderness can be serious, simply because you cannot quickly reach skilled medical help. Ingenuity and cool judgment will be your best friends. Do not panic, but try to think carefully what to do and how to do it. Speed is usually important in emergencies. Do not forget to appeal to Jesus, the Great Physician, for help. The age of miracles is not past.

CHAPTER 21

WILDERNESS PESTS

Whether you are out in the wilderness, in a primitive camp, or even in a modern camp, the problem of pests is ever present. Mosquitoes, flies, ants, and chiggers are the most common offenders.

YOUR CAMP

The location of your camp is vital as the first consideration in pest control, especially if mosquitoes are about. Do not camp too close to a lake or a creek or in a dense forest. The farther you can get from nonrunning water the better. Make your camp in a high meadow, or on an open ridge, or near a small clear spring if possible. Choose a high point in the open where the wind will carry the flies and mosquitoes away. If you camp in a tent, screened door and windows are a must if you want to enjoy camping where mosquitoes abound.

MOSQUITO NETTING

If camping in a tent, a veteran camper has suggested that you have a full net sewed to the junction of the front and the walls of your tent in such a way that it will fall in a loose drape long enough for at least a foot of it to lie along the floor cloth. All you do is lift the net, walk in or out, and let it drop after you. When you do not need the net, use the tapes to hold it up out of the way. However, most modern tents have these nets already sewed into both the door flap and the windows.

Sleeping bags should have mosquito bars, with the

bottom edge of the net tucked under the bag. You can drive thin, flexible poles into the ground on both sides of the sleeping bag to form an arc. Cover this framework with a large piece of cheesecloth, with the material draped on the ground at least a foot all around.

You can purchase in sporting-goods stores mosquito nets that droop from the broad brim of a hat over your face and head. They either tuck in at the neck or (preferably) extend over the shoulders and tie under the arms. Such gear is unnecessary around most camps, but you may welcome it on a pack trip in an isolated area in which you plan to camp at least overnight, for exploring, or even for traveling through mosquito-infested country. In addition, you may need to wear leather gloves for protection.

MOSQUITOES

You are not too apt to come in contact with the Anopheles mosquito, which carries the malaria parasite, or the *Aedes aegypti* mosquito, which spreads yellow fever, but it is possible. Any mosquito can make you very uncomfortable. As stated before, locate your camp away from the edge of a brook, a lakeshore, or thick woods. Camp higher up and as far from nonrunning water as is convenient. Pitch your camp in the open air where the wind will carry mosquitoes away or on a point of land extending well into open water. A good site is on a high-cut bank above a mountain river, or on an open ridge, or in a high meadow near a small, clear spring.

To get rid of mosquitoes without the usual sprays or repellents is not easy in the wilderness. A smudge fire of damp, green wood and moist vegetation is quite effective. Drain all stagnant water in pools without outlets. Protect yourself with netting if at all possible, covering your neck and ankles. Pad the inside of your clothing with leaves and thin strips of bark. Keep your clothing loose except at the wrists and ankles. Avoid scratching bites lest they become infected.

FLIES

Flies can be about as bothersome as mosquitoes. Some are active at night, others in the daytime. Some are vicious biters—the black flies, especially. Flies carry such diseases as typhoid, cholera, tuberculosis, anthrax, yaws, and trachoma on their feet. When they subsequently land on food, they contaminate it. We have all seen them land on human or animal excreta and other refuse and garbage. Cover carefully all food as well as cooking and eating utensils. Cover deposits in latrines and garbage pits with dirt or ashes at once. Either burn or bury garbage. Smudge fires are also effective against flies.

ANTS

A clean camp usually remains free from ants. Spilled foods, especially cooked food or honey, entice this little pest to become your guest. If you have ant powder or spray, you are indeed fortunate. However, when in the wilderness, watch where you make camp so that you do not unwittingly place your cooking area in the path of ants. Watch out for anthills. Cleanliness is your greatest factor in avoiding these little insects.

CHIGGERS

Chiggers are mites, the larvae of Trombicula and Entrombicula. They are so small that they are difficult to see with the naked eye. They penetrate inside the clothing. Their bite turns bright red about the size of the head of a pin, and the area becomes irritated and swollen, usually developing water blisters. Their bite is not very painful but itches when scratched. Avoid scratching, however, because of the danger of infection. If you should scratch chigger bites, you are in for trouble. Wash the area with strong soap if you have it. A hot bath and soapy lather relieve the irritation. One veteran camper has suggested that before you go into an area in which you suspect chiggers, you should rub your wrists, neck, ankles, and abdomen with kerosene.

WOOD TICKS

Tick bites can be serious and in some cases have been fatal. The wood tick transmits Rocky Mountain spotted fever and tularemia. The former is an infectious disease caused by a parasite the wood tick transmits. Tularemia is a deer fly fever transmitted to man from rodents by the wood tick or by direct contact. Fever, pains in bones and muscles, and profuse reddish eruption mark Rocky Mountain spotted fever. Tularemia has the following symptoms: Three days after infection, the person develops a headache, chilliness, vomiting, aching pains, and fever. The site of infection usually develops into an ulcer. Glands at the elbow or in the armpit may become enlarged, tender, and painful.

Many times ticks and chiggers are found together and are especially bothersome in spring and summer. They cling to the tops of tall grass and weeds and the underside of leaves, then drop on unsuspecting travelers. They fasten themselves tenaciously to the skin, but they do not generally dig their heads in and begin to suck blood until several hours after getting onto the body. You can detect them by daily inspection. When examining for ticks, look at the base of the head and hairy portions of the body, under the arms and groin.

Do not attempt to pull or unscrew them, as you may not get the head out. Pass a sharp knife between them and your skin to remove them. If they have taken a firm hold, the heat from a match or burning ember placed near them will cause them to back out—and sometimes even to explode! Intense smoke or hot water may also cause them to back out and drop off. If available, a drop of kerosene or alcohol is effective.

STINGS FROM BEES, WASPS, AND YELLOW JACKETS

Honeybee, large bumblebee, wasp, and yellow jacket stings are very painful. Some people are highly allergic and can even die if stung numerous times. If you know you are allergic, carry an antihistamine, or whatever your doctor prescribes, with you whenever you go out of reach of medical help. Some Indian tribes crushed the stems and leaves of jewelweed, also known as touch-me-not (*Impatiens aurea, biflora*), and made them into poultices, which they placed on the bites. Mud poultices have given relief to some by soothing and taking the swelling down. Some Indians also used the juice from leaves of climbing hempweed (*Apocynum cannabinum*) for stings.

BLACK WIDOW SPIDERS

The female is the dangerous one in this family. She has a red spot on her abdomen about the shape of an hourglass. Her poison is even more potent and dangerous than that of the rattlesnake. Her bite consists of two small red dots surrounded by a white area. The site of the bite will swell slightly. High temperature, severe aches and pains, stomach cramps, dizziness, and nausea follow her bite. The person bitten must be reassured and put to bed at once. Frequent hot baths are said to help, but not much can be done without the injection of calcium gluconate, 10 cc. in a 10 percent solution, intravenously. Try to seek medical help at once. If completely isolated, remember to call upon the Great Physician.

CENTIPEDES AND SCORPIONS

The bite of all centipedes is poisonous but rarely serious. The centipede is usually found under logs, stones, or leaves. They prey on insects and spiders. Be sure to shake your clothing and shoes before putting them on. Also inspect your bedding before retiring. The centipede loves to hide in these things.

The scorpion sting is much like that of the wasp or yellow jacket. It causes a sharp, stinging pain, and a white circle forms around the place stung. The sting is extremely painful but usually goes away in about thirty minutes. If you are stung early in the spring before the scorpion has had a chance to use its poison, and if the scorpion happens to be of a dangerous species, you may experience numbness, itching of nose and throat, an excessive amount of saliva, collapse, or perhaps convulsions. As a rule recovery follows, but occasionally a scorpion sting may have fatal results.

Scorpions hide in the daytime and are active at night. They may hide in your shoes or clothing to escape from the light, so be sure to shake out your clothing before wearing. Scorpions sting with their tail spine and usually only when molested.

CHAPTER 22

KEEPING UP MORALE

SPIRITUAL UPLIFT AND ENCOURAGEMENT

When you have spent your entire life in the city, with a supermarket and other stores just around the corner and a home filled with laborsaving devices, it will be a drastic change to find yourself having to live in the wilderness. You will have to use primitive methods of fire making, cooking, washing, and bathing; and hundreds of other chores will have to be done the hard way. You will have no radio (unless you have along a little transistor), no TV, no entertainment except that offered by nature herself. Life will be simple, but this does not mean that you should go around with a long face, moping and feeling sorry for yourself. On the contrary, this is the time to face the challenge before you. Be courageous, and take a positive attitude toward your situation. "A merry heart doeth good like a medicine." Proverbs 17:22.

Tell yourself that you are now living in the wilderness and that you can and will make a success of it. This book will help enable you to get acquainted with wild foods and will teach you how to make a warm shelter, how to make a fire under adverse circumstances, and how to find water. You *will* survive, and in time you will even live fairly comfortably. So face up to it, and you will find yourself actually enjoying yourself! "I will go in the strength of the Lord." Psalm 71:16.

It is very important that you develop complete trust in God. He will supply your needs. "My God shall sup-

ply all your need according to his riches in glory by
Christ Jesus." Philippians 4:19. Trust in His divine
protection. "The righteous cry, and the Lord heareth,
and delivereth them out of all their troubles." Psalm
34:17. Establish morning and evening devotions. Spend
time each day reading the Scriptures, for they contain
literally hundreds of precious promises. *Now* is the time
to strengthen your faith. When you read a promise, believe it with all your heart. If you believe that God
exists, you must also believe that He means what He
says. You will live on naked faith in the wilderness.
Start claiming His promises right now.

The United States Air Force Manual, *Emergency
Rescue Survival,* includes a whole section of Bible texts
and readings for Protestants, Catholics, and Jews. It is,
therefore, proper for this book to include some Bible
promises and quotations from Ellen G. White which will
give you encouragement and spiritual uplift for the days
ahead, especially if you find yourself without a Bible
and concordance.

FOOD, WATER, AND SHELTER

1. "Can God furnish a table in the wilderness?"
Psalm 78:19. *Answer:* "The wilderness yieldeth food for
them and for their children." Job 24:5. Also: "From His
resources He can spread a table in the wilderness."—
Prophets and Kings, p. 242.

2. "My people are destroyed for lack of knowledge."
Hosea 4:6. *Note:* We must do our part by studying how
to help ourselves *now.*

3. "And God said, Behold, I have given you every
herb bearing seed, which is upon the face of all the
earth, and every tree, in the which is the fruit of a tree
yielding seed; to you it shall be for meat." Genesis 1:29.

4. "He causeth the grass to grow for the cattle, and
herb for the service of man: that he may bring forth food
out of the earth." Psalm 104:14.

5. "Thou shalt eat the herb of the field." Genesis 3:18.

6. "The hay appeareth, and the tender grass sheweth itself, and herbs of the mountains are gathered." Proverbs 27:25.

7. "And one went out into the field to gather herbs." 2 Kings 4:39.

8. "I will even make a way in the wilderness, and rivers in the desert, . . . because I give waters in the wilderness, and rivers in the desert, to give drink to my people, my chosen." Isaiah 43:19, 20.

9. "I will pour water upon him that is thirsty, and floods upon the dry ground: . . . and they shall spring up as among the grass, as willows by the water courses." Isaiah 44:3, 4.

10. "They shall dwell safely in the wilderness, and sleep in the woods." Ezekiel 34:25.

11. "He shall dwell on high: his place of defence shall be the munitions of rocks: bread shall be given him; his waters shall be sure." Isaiah 33:16.

THE LORD WILL HEAR YOUR CRY

1. "Whosoever shall call upon the name of the Lord shall be saved." Romans 10:13.

2. "Call unto me, and I will answer thee, and shew thee great and mighty things, which thou knowest not." Jeremiah 33:3.

3. "He shall call upon me, and I will answer him: I will be with him in trouble; I will deliver him, and honour him." Psalm 91:15.

4. "The Lord is nigh unto all them that call upon him, to all that call upon him in truth." Psalm 145:18.

5. "Then shalt thou call, and the Lord shall answer; thou shalt cry, and he shall say, Here I am." Isaiah 58:9.

6. "It shall come to pass, that before they call, I will answer; and while they are yet speaking, I will hear." Isaiah 65:24.

7. "Then shall ye call upon me, and ye shall go and pray unto me, and I will hearken unto you. And ye shall seek me, and find me, when ye shall search for me

with all your heart." Jeremiah 29:12, 13.

8. "Thou shalt weep no more: he will be very gracious unto thee at the voice of thy cry; when he shall hear it, he will answer thee." Isaiah 30:19.

9. "The righteous cry, and the Lord heareth, and delivereth them out of all their troubles. The Lord is nigh unto them that are of a broken heart; and saveth such as be of a contrite spirit." Psalm 34:17, 18.

10. "Ask, and it shall be given you; seek, and ye shall find; knock, and it shall be opened unto you." Matthew 7:7; Luke 11:9.

11. "Whatsoever we ask, we receive of him, because we keep his commandments, and do those things that are pleasing in his sight." 1 John 3:22.

12. "If we ask any thing according to his will, he heareth us." 1 John 5:14.

13. "If two of you shall agree on earth as touching any thing that they shall ask, it shall be done for them of my Father which is in heaven." Matthew 18:19.

14. "All things, whatsoever ye shall ask in prayer, believing, ye shall receive." Matthew 21:22.

15. "If ye abide in me, and my words abide in you, ye shall ask what ye will, and it shall be done unto you." John 15:7.

16. "What things soever ye desire, when ye pray, believe that ye receive them, and ye shall have them." Mark 11:24.

THE LORD WILL HELP YOU AND DELIVER YOU

1. "Thou art my hiding place; thou shalt preserve me from trouble; thou shalt compass me about with songs of deliverance." Psalm 32:7.

2. "Fear thou not; for I am with thee: be not dismayed; for I am thy God: I will strengthen thee; yea, I will help thee; yea, I will uphold thee with the right hand of my righteousness." Isaiah 41:10.

3. "The Lord God will help me; therefore shall I not be confounded." Isaiah 50:7.

4. "God is our refuge and strength, a very present help in trouble." Psalm 46:1.

5. "I will contend with him that contendeth with thee." Isaiah 49:25.

6. "They shall fight against thee; but they shall not prevail against thee; for I am with thee, saith the Lord, to deliver thee." Jeremiah 1:19.

7. "No weapon that is formed against thee shall prosper; and every tongue that shall rise against thee in judgment thou shalt condemn. This is the heritage of the servants of the Lord." Isaiah 54:17.

8. "Behold, all they that were incensed against thee shall be ashamed and confounded: they shall be as nothing; and they that strive with thee shall perish." Isaiah 41:11.

9. "Be not afraid of their faces: for I am with thee to deliver thee, saith the Lord." Jeremiah 1:8.

10. "The Lord also will be a refuge for the oppressed, a refuge in times of trouble." Psalm 9:9.

"TRUST IN THE LORD"

1. "Blessed is the man that trusteth in the Lord, and whose hope the Lord is. For he shall be as a tree planted by the waters, and that spreadeth out her roots by the river, and shall not see when heat cometh, but her leaf shall be green." Jeremiah 17:7, 8.

2. "Trust in the Lord, and do good; so shalt thou dwell in the land, and verily thou shalt be fed." Psalm 37:3.

3. "Commit thy way unto the Lord; trust also in him; and he shall bring it to pass." Psalm 37:5.

THE LORD WILL GUIDE YOU

1. "I will instruct thee and teach thee in the way which thou shalt go: I will guide thee with mine eye." Psalm 32:8.

2. "In all thy ways acknowledge him, and he shall direct thy paths." Proverbs 3:6.

3. "For this God is our God for ever and ever: he will be our guide even unto death." Psalm 48:14.

4. "The Lord shall guide thee continually." Isaiah 58:11.

5. "Thou shalt guide me with thy counsel, and afterward receive me to glory." Psalm 73:24.

"BE STRONG AND OF A GOOD COURAGE"

1. "I will be with thee: I will not fail thee, nor forsake thee. Be strong and of a good courage. . . . Only be thou strong and very courageous, that thou mayest observe to do according to all the law: . . . turn not from it to the right hand or to the left, that thou mayest prosper whithersoever thou goest, . . . that thou mayest observe to do according to all that is written therein: for then thou shalt make thy way prosperous, and then thou shalt have good success. . . . Be strong and of a good courage; be not afraid, neither be thou dismayed: for the Lord thy God is with thee whithersoever thou goest." Joshua 1:5-9.

2. "Fear not, nor be dismayed, be strong and of good courage." Joshua 10:25.

WAIT PATIENTLY ON THE LORD

1. "Wait on the Lord: be of good courage, and he shall strengthen thine heart: wait, I say, on the Lord." Psalm 27:14.

2. "It is good that a man should both hope and quietly wait for the salvation of the Lord." Lamentations 3:26.

3. "Rest in the Lord, and wait patiently for him." Psalm 37:7.

4. "Those that wait upon the Lord, they shall inherit the earth." Psalm 37:9.

HE WILL GIVE US THE DESIRES OF OUR HEART

1. "Thou hast given him his heart's desire, and hast not withholden the request of his lips." Psalm 21:2.

2. "He will fulfil the desire of them that fear him:

he will also hear their cry, and will save them." Psalm 145:19.

3. "Delight thyself also in the Lord: and he shall give thee the desires of thine heart. Commit thy way unto the Lord; trust also in him; and he shall bring it to pass." Psalm 37:4, 5.

4. "The desire of the righteous shall be granted." Proverbs 10:24. "The desire of the righteous is only good." Proverbs 11:23.

5. "They that seek the Lord shall not want any good thing." Psalm 34:10.

6. "Thou openest thine hand, and satisfiest the desire of every living thing." Psalm 145:16.

7. "No good thing will he withhold from them that walk uprightly." Psalm 84:11.

HE WILL FORGIVE OUR SINS

1. "I have blotted out, as a thick cloud, thy transgressions, and, as a cloud, thy sins: return unto me; for I have redeemed thee." Isaiah 44:22.

2. "I, even I, am he that blotteth out thy transgressions for mine own sake, and will not remember thy sins." Isaiah 43:25.

3. "If we confess our sins, he is faithful and just to forgive us our sins, and to cleanse us from all unrighteousness." 1 John 1:9.

4. "He hath not dealt with us after our sins; nor rewarded us according to our iniquities. . . . As far as the east is from the west, so far hath he removed our transgressions from us. . . . He knoweth our frame, he remembereth that we are dust." Psalm 103:10-14.

HE WILL HEAL OUR DISEASES AND GIVE US HEALTH

1. "I will restore health unto thee, and I will heal thee of thy wounds." Jeremiah 30:17.

2. "Who forgiveth all thine iniquities; who healeth

all thy diseases." Psalm 103:3.

3. "If thou wilt diligently hearken to the voice of the Lord thy God, and wilt do that which is right in his sight, and wilt give ear to his commandments, and keep all his statutes, I will put none of these diseases upon thee, which I have brought upon the Egyptians: for I am the Lord that healeth thee." Exodus 15:26.

4. "The Lord will take away from thee all sickness, and will put none of the evil diseases of Egypt, which thou knowest, upon thee." Deuteronomy 7:15.

OUR REWARD

1. "Since the beginning of the world men have not heard, nor perceived by the ear, neither hath the eye seen, O God, beside thee, what he hath prepared for him that waiteth for him." Isaiah 64:4.

2. "But as it is written, Eye hath not seen, nor ear heard, neither have entered into the heart of man, the things which God hath prepared for them that love him." 1 Corinthians 2:9.

3. "The wolf also shall dwell with the lamb, and the leopard shall lie down with the kid; and the calf and the young lion and the fatling together; and a little child shall lead them. And the cow and the bear shall feed; their young ones shall lie down together: and the lion shall eat straw like the ox. . . . They shall not hurt nor destroy in all my holy mountain." Isaiah 11:6-9.

4. "For, behold, I create new heavens and a new earth: and the former shall not be remembered, nor come into mind. . . . And the voice of weeping shall be no more heard in her, nor the voice of crying. . . . They shall build houses, and inhabit them; and they shall plant vineyards, and eat the fruit of them. . . . The wolf and the lamb shall feed together, and the lion shall eat straw like the bullock. . . . They shall not hurt nor destroy in all my holy mountain, saith the Lord." Isaiah 65:17-25.

5. "And I saw a new heaven and a new earth: for the first heaven and the first earth were passed away. . . .

And God shall wipe away all tears from their eyes; and there shall be no more death, neither sorrow, nor crying, neither shall there be any more pain: for the former things are passed away. . . . Behold, I make all things new." Revelation 21:1-5.

6. "And he shewed me a pure river of water of life, clear as crystal, proceeding out of the throne of God and of the Lamb. In the midst of the street of it, and on either side of the river, was there the tree of life, which bare twelve manner of fruits, and yielded her fruit every month: and the leaves of the tree were for the healing of the nations. . . . And they shall see his face; and his name shall be in their foreheads." "Blessed are they that do his commandments, that they may have right to the tree of life, and may enter in through the gates into the city." Revelation 22:1-4, 14.

THE TWENTY-THIRD PSALM

"The Lord is my shepherd; I shall not want. He maketh me to lie down in green pastures: he leadeth me beside the still waters. He restoreth my soul: he leadeth me in the paths of righteousness for his name's sake. Yea, though I walk through the valley of the shadow of death, I will fear no evil: for thou art with me; thy rod and thy staff they comfort me. Thou preparest a table before me in the presence of mine enemies; thou anointest my head with oil; my cup runneth over. Surely goodness and mercy shall follow me all the days of my life: and I will dwell in the house of the Lord for ever."

THE NINETY-FIRST PSALM

"He that dwelleth in the secret place of the most High shall abide under the shadow of the Almighty.

"I will say of the Lord, He is my refuge and my fortress: my God; in him will I trust. Surely he shall deliver thee from the snare of the fowler, and from the noisome pestilence. He shall cover thee with his feathers, and under his wings shalt thou trust: his truth shall be thy shield and buckler.

"Thou shalt not be afraid for the terror by night; nor for the arrow that flieth by day; nor for the pestilence that walketh in darkness; nor for the destruction that wasteth at noonday. A thousand shall fall at thy side, and ten thousand at thy right hand; but it shall not come nigh thee.

"Only with thine eyes shalt thou behold and see the reward of the wicked. Because thou hast made the Lord, which is my refuge, even the most High, thy habitation; there shall no evil befall thee, neither shall any plague come nigh thy dwelling. For he shall give his angels charge over thee, to keep thee in all thy ways. They shall bear thee up in their hands, lest thou dash thy foot against a stone. Thou shalt tread upon the lion and adder: the young lion and the dragon shalt thou trample under feet.

"Because he hath set his love upon me, therefore will I deliver him: I will set him on high, because he hath known my name. He shall call upon me, and I will answer him: I will be with him in trouble; I will deliver him, and honour him. With long life will I satisfy him, and shew him my salvation."

QUOTATIONS ON FOOD, WATER, AND SHELTER

1. "Under His direction *food will go a long way*. When we place ourselves in right relation to Him, He will help us, and the food we eat in obedience to Him will satisfy us. *We can subsist on very much less than we think we can,* if God's blessing is on the food; and if it is for His glory, He can *multiply* it."—*Counsels on Health,* p. 495. (Italics supplied.)

2. "He who created man, who gave him his wonderful physical, mental, and spiritual faculties, will not withhold that which is necessary to sustain the life He has given. He who has given us His word—the leaves of

the tree of life—*will not withhold from us a knowledge of how to provide food for His needy children.*"—*The Ministry of Healing,* p. 199. (Italics supplied.)

3. "From His resources He can spread a table in the wilderness."—*Prophets and Kings,* p. 242.

4. "God is working in behalf of His people. *He does not desire them to be without resources.* He is bringing them back to the diet originally given to man. Their diet is to consist of the foods made from the materials He has provided. The materials principally used in these foods will be fruits and grains and nuts, but various roots will also be used."—*Counsels on Diet and Foods,* pp. 81, 82. (Italics supplied.)

5. "Our heavenly Father has a thousand ways to provide for us of which we know nothing. Those who accept the one principle of making the service of God supreme, will find perplexities vanish and a plain path before their feet."—*The Ministry of Healing,* p. 481.

6. "But the earth has blessings hidden in her depths for those who have courage and will and perseverance to gather her treasures."—*Fundamentals of Christian Education,* pp. 326, 327.

7. "With proper, intelligent cultivation the earth will yield its treasures for the benefit of man. The mountains and hills are changing; the earth is waxing old like a garment; *but the blessing of God, which spreads a table for His people in the wilderness, will never cease.*"—*Testimonies,* Vol. 6, p. 178. (Italics supplied.)

FOR FURTHER READING

Books

American Red Cross, The, *First Aid*. Garden City, New York: Doubleday and Company, Inc., 1965. $1.25.

ANGIER, BRADFORD, *Free for the Eating*. Harrisburg, Pennsylvania: Stackpole Books, 1966. $4.95.

————, *Living Off the Country: How to Stay Alive in the Woods*. Harrisburg, Pennsylvania: Stackpole Books, 1959. $5.00.

————, *More Free-for-the-Eating Wild Foods*. Harrisburg, Pennsylvania: Stackpole Books, 1969. $4.95.

ARMSTRONG, MARGARET, and THORBER, J. J., *Field Book of Western Wild Flowers*. New York: G. P. Putnam's Sons, 1915.

Boy Scouts of America, *Boy Scout Handbook*. New Brunswick, New Jersey, 1962. $1.00.

COON, NELSON, *Using Wayside Plants*. New York: Hearthside Press, Inc., 1960. $5.95.

CRAIGHEAD, FRANK C., JR., and CRAIGHEAD, JOHN J., *How to Survive on Land and Sea*. Annapolis, Maryland: U.S. Naval Institute, 1965. $4.50.

DARNALL, JACK and MIRIAM, *Wilderness Survival Seminars Field Manual*. Portland, Tennessee, 1967. $3.50.

Department of Defense, *In Time of Emergency*. Office of Civil Defense, March, 1968.

Department of the Air Force, *Emergency Rescue Survival, Air Force Manual*. Washington, D.C.: Division of Public Documents, U.S. Government Printing Office, 1961. $1.00.

DRAKE, HAROLD A., *Common Edible Wild Plants*. South Lancaster, Massachusetts: College Press, 1957.

Dreisbach, Robert H., *Handbook of Poisoning: Diagnosis and Treatment*. Los Altos, California: Lange Medical Publications, 1961. (Pages 351-367.) $6.00.

Gibbons, Euell, *Stalking the Healthful Herbs*. New York: David McKay Company, Inc., 1966. $7.50.

————, *Stalking the Wild Asparagus*. New York: David McKay Company, Inc., 1962. $7.95.

Hammett, Catherine T., *Your Own Book of Campcraft*. New York: Pocket Books, Inc., 1961.   60¢.

Jaeger, Ellsworth, *Wildwood Wisdom*. New York: The Macmillan Company, 1966. $5.95.

Jepson, Willis Linn, *A Manual of the Flowering Plants of California*. Berkeley, California: University of California Press, 1966. $10.00.

Kesting, Ted, *The Outdoor Encyclopedia*. Cranbury, New Jersey: A. S. Barnes and Company, 1957. $7.50.

Kirk, Donald R., *Wild Edible Plants of the Western United States*. Healdsburg, California: Naturegraph Company, 1970. $3.95.

Kreps, E., *Camp and Trail Methods*. Columbus, Ohio: A. R. Harding, 1910.

Maxwell, Lawrence, *Pathfinder Field Guide*. Washington, D.C.: Review and Herald Publishing Association, 1962.

Medsger, Oliver Perry, *Edible Wild Plants*. New York: The Macmillan Company, 1966. $7.50.

Mitchell, A. Viola, and Crawford, Ida B., *Camp Counseling*. Philadelphia: W. B. Saunders Company, 1961. $6.25.

Murphy, Edith Van Allen, *Indian Uses of Native Plants*. Fort Bragg, California: Mendocino County Historical Society, 1959. $2.65.

Nesbitt, Paul H., Pond, Alonzo W., and Allen, William H., *The Survival Book*. New York: Funk and Wagnalls, 1969. $1.95.

Robbins, W. W., Bellue, Margaret K., and Ball, Walter S., *Weeds of California*. Sacramento, California: State Department of Agriculture, 1941. $1.75.

Rutstrum, Calvin, *The New Way of the Wilderness.* New York: The Macmillan Company, 1966. $4.95.

Smith, Alexander H., *The Mushroom Hunter's Field Guide.* Ann Arbor, Michigan: The University of Michigan Press, 1963. $8.95.

Spencer, Edwin Rollin, *Just Weeds.* New York: Charles Scribner's Sons, 1957. $6.00.

Sweet, Muriel, *Common Edible and Useful Plants of the West.* Healdsburg, California: Naturegraph Company, 1962. $3.50; paper, $1.50.

Whelen, Townsend, and Angier, Bradford, *On Your Own in the Wilderness.* Harrisburg, Pennsylvania: Stackpole Books, 1963. $5.00.

White, Ellen G., *Country Living.* Washington, D.C.: Review and Herald Publishing Association, 1946.

————, *From City to Country Living.* Washington, D.C.: Review and Herald Publishing Association, 1950.

Pamphlets

Let's Plant Seeds of Safety. Interdepartmental Safety Committee, Pacific Telephone Northwest.

Poison Ivy, Poison Oak, and Poison Sumac. Washington, D.C.: Farmer's Bulletin No. 1972, U.S. Department of Agriculture, 1963.

Tucker, J. M., Fowler, M. E., Harvey, W. A., and Berry, L. J., *Poisonous Hemlocks.* Circular 530, California Agricultural Experimental Station, University of California, Berkeley, California, October, 1964.

Tucker, John M., and Kimball, M. H., *Poisonous Plants in the Garden.* Agricultural Extension Service, University of California, 1960.

FOOD ANALYSIS CHART

100 Grams Edible Portion

Food	% Water	gm. Protein	gm. Fat	gm. Carbohyd.	mg. Calcium	mg. Phos.	mg. Iron	mg. Sodium	mg. Potassium	IU Vitamin A	mg. Vitamin C	Calories
Bamboo shoots	91.0	2.6	0.3	5.2	13	59	0.5	—	533	20	4	27
Beechnuts	6.6	19.4	50.0	20.3	—	—	—	—	170	200	21	568
Blackberries	84.5	1.2	0.9	12.9	32	19	0.9	1	170	200	21	58
Blueberries	83.2	0.7	0.5	15.3	15	13	1.0	1	81	100	14	62
Butternuts	3.8	23.7	61.2	8.4	—	—	6.8	—	—	—	—	629
Carob flour (St. John's bread)	11.2	4.5	1.4	80.7	352	81	—	—	—	—	—	180
Chestnuts	52.5	2.9	1.5	42.1	27	88	1.7	6	454	—	—	194
Chicory greens	92.8	1.8	0.3	3.8	86	40	0.9	—	420	4,000	22	20
Corn salad, raw	92.8	2.0	0.4	3.6	—	—	—	—	—	—	—	21
Cranberries	87.9	0.4	0.7	10.8	14	10	0.5	2	82	40	11	46
Cress, water	89.4	2.6	0.7	5.5	81	76	1.3	14	606	9,300	69	32
Currants	84.2	1.7	0.1	13.1	60	40	1.1	3	372	230	200	54
Dandelion greens (cooked)	89.8	2.2	0.6	6.4	140	42	1.8	44	232	11,700	18	33
Dock, curly, cooked	93.6	1.6	0.2	3.9	55	26	0.9	3	198	10,800	54	19
Elderberries	79.8	2.6	0.5	16.4	38	28	1.6	—	300	600	36	72
Fennel, raw leaves	90.0	2.8	0.4	5.1	100	51	2.7	—	397	3,500	31	28
Garlic	61.3	6.2	0.2	30.8	29	202	1.5	19	529	trace	15	137
Gooseberries	88.9	0.8	0.2	9.7	18	15	0.5	1	155	290	33	39
Ground-cherries	85.4	1.9	0.7	11.2	9	40	1.0	—	—	720	11	53

Hazelnuts	5.8	12.6	62.4	16.7	209	337	3.4	2	704	—	trace	634
Hickory nuts	3.3	13.2	68.7	12.8	trace	360	2.4	—	—	—	—	673
Horseradish	74.6	3.2	0.3	19.7	140	64	1.4	8	564	—	81	87
Jerusalem artichokes	79.8	2.3	0.1	16.7	14	78	3.4	—	—	20	4	75
Lamb's-quarters (cooked)	88.9	3.2	0.7	5.0	258	45	0.7	—	—	9,700	37	32
Millet, whole grain	11.8	9.9	2.9	72.9	20	311	6.8	—	430	—	—	327
Mushrooms	90.4	2.7	0.3	4.4	6	116	0.8	15	414	trace	3	28
Mustard greens (cooked)	92.6	2.2	0.4	4.0	138	32	1.8	18	220	5,800	48	23
Oyster plant (salsify) (cooked)	81.0	2.6	0.6	15.1	42	53	1.3	—	226	10	7	82
Plantain	66.4	1.1	0.4	31.2	7	30	0.7	5	385	1,200	14	119
Pokeweed (cooked)	92.9	2.2	0.4	3.1	53	33	1.2	—	—	8,700	82	20
Prickly pears, raw	88.0	0.5	0.1	10.9	20	28	0.3	2	166	60	22	42
Purslane (cooked)	94.7	1.2	0.3	2.8	86	24	1.2	—	—	2,100	12	15
Sheep sorrel (cooked)	93.6	1.6	0.2	3.9	55	26	0.9	3	198	10,800	54	19
Strawberries	89.9	0.7	0.5	8.4	21	21	1.0	1	164	60	59	37
Sunflower seeds, dry	4.8	24.0	47.3	19.9	120	837	7.1	30	920	50	—	560
Walnuts, black	3.1	20.5	59.3	14.8	trace	570	6.0	3	460	300	—	628
Wild rice, raw	8.5	14.1	0.7	75.3	19	339	4.2	7	220	—	—	353

Note: These figures were taken from "Composition of Foods," Agriculture Handbook No. 8, Agriculture Research Service, United States Department of Agriculture, Washington, D.C. Revised December 1963.
Abbreviations used: gm.—gram; mg.—milligram; IU—International Unit; Phos.—phosphorus.

INDEX

* Numbers in italics indicate page on which illustration is found.